Keto

For Carb Lovers For Beginners

The 5-Ingredient Fresh and Easy Cookbook: 100+ Recipes For Busy People Who Love to Eat Well

Tiffany Moon

Table of Contents

INTRODUCTION		6
BREAKFAST		8
1.	Peanut Butter Cup Smoothie	8
2.	Berry Green Smoothie	8
3.	Lemon-Cashew Smoothie	8
4.	Spinach-Blueberry Smoothie	8
5.	Creamy Cinnamon Smoothie	9
6.	Nut Medley Granola	9
7.	Bacon-Artichoke Omelet	9
8.	Mushroom Frittata	10
9.	Breakfast Bake	10
10.	Avocado And Eggs	11
MAINS		12
11.	Verde Chicken Enchiladas	12
12.	"K.F.C." Keto Fried Chicken	12
13.	Turkey Taco Boats	13
14.	Alex's "Chick And Brock" Casserole	13
15.	Stuffed Chicken For Suppah	13
16.	Silky Chicken With Mushroom Sauce	14
17.	Indoor Bbq Chicken	14
18.	Chipotle Chicken Fajita Bowl	15
19.	Fluffy Chicken	15
20.	N'awlins Chicken	16
21.	Four Horsemen Butter Chicken	16
SIDES		18
22.	Cheesy Bacon & Eggplant Gratin	18
23.	Wrapped Halloumi in Bacon	18
24.	Sweet Mustard Mini Sausages	18
25.	Chili Broccoli & Pancetta Roast	19
26.	Chili Turnip Fries	19
27.	Buttery Radish & Minute Steak Sauté	19
28.	Cheddar Bacon & Celeriac Bake	19
29.	Easy Bacon & Cheese Balls	20
SEAFOOD		21
30.	Cheesy Tuna Pâté	21
31.	Cheesy Salmon Dip	21

32.	Easy Halibut Steaks	21
33.	Cholula Shrimp Spread	21
34.	Sherry and Butter Prawns	22
35.	Super Easy Fish Cakes	22
36.	Zingy Tuna Steaks with Spinach	22
37.	Clams with Garlic-Tomato Sauce	23
38.	Amberjack Fillets with Cheese Sauce	23
39.	Refreshing Prawn Salad	24
40.	Middle-Eastern Salmon with Nabulsi Cheese	24
41.	Red Snapper Soup	24
42.	Family Seafood Bowl	25
43.	Tilapia with Spicy Dijon Sauce	25
44.	Rich and Spicy Seafood Stew	25

POULTRY — 27

45.	Bacon-Wrapped Chicken with Grilled Asparagus	27
46.	Spinach Chicken Cheesy Bake	27
47.	Parmesan Wings with Yogurt Sauce	27
48.	Eggplant & Tomato Braised Chicken Thighs	28
49.	Lemon Threaded Chicken Skewers	28
50.	Creamy Stuffed Chicken with Parma Ham	29
51.	Chicken Drumsticks in Tomato Sauce	29
52.	Chicken, Broccoli & Cashew Stir-Fry	30
53.	Cheese Stuffed Chicken Breasts with Spinach	30
54.	Chili Turkey Patties with Cucumber Salsa	31

MEAT — 32

55.	Lemon Butter Pork Chops	32
56.	Fully Loaded Burger Bowls	32
57.	Roasted Lamb Rack	33
58.	Braised Beef Brisket	33
59.	Beef Chuck Roast	33
60.	Saucy Pernil Pork	34
61.	Creamy Pork Tenderloin	34
62.	Italian Sausage Satay	35
63.	Seasoned Pork Chops	35
64.	Garlicky Pork Roast	35
65.	Spiced Pork Tenderloin	36
66.	Basil-Rubbed Pork Chops	36

VEGETABLES — 37

67.	Grilled Sandwich Cheese	37
68.	New Basil Pizza With Paprika	37
69.	Splendid Jalapeno Poppers	37
70.	Personal Pizzas In Portobello	38
71.	Green Vegetarian Coconut Curry	38
72.	Pork Shiitake With "Fast Kimchi" Stir Fry	39
73.	Avocado Stuffed With Egg Salad	39
74.	Cheesy Waffles With Thyme	40
75.	Simple Omelet Recette	40

SOUPS AND STEWS — 41

76.	Chicken Cabbage Soup	41
77.	Corn and Bacon Chowder	41
78.	Creamy Cauliflower Soup	41
79.	Tomato Hamburger Soup	41
80.	Bacon Chowder	42
81.	Mexican Soup	42
82.	Mushroom Soup	43
83.	Rustic Beef Soup	43
84.	Coconut Cauliflower Soup	43
85.	Clam Chowder	43

SNACKS — 45

86.	Buttery Slow-Cooker Mushrooms	45
87.	Parmesan And Pork Rind Green Beans	45
88.	Crunchy Pork Rind Zucchini Sticks	45
89.	Keto Bread	46
90.	Chicken-Pecan Salad Cucumber Bites	46
91.	Buffalo Chicken Dip	46
92.	Roasted Brussels Sprouts With Bacon	47
93.	Salami, Pepperoncini, And Cream Cheese Pinwheels	47
94.	Bacon-Wrapped Jalapeños	48
95.	Creamy Broccoli-Bacon Salad	48
96.	Cauliflower Steaks With Bacon And Blue Cheese	49
97.	Cauliflower "Potato" Salad	49

DESSERTS — 50

98.	Coconut Bombs	50
99.	Raspberry Cheesecake	50
100.	Keto Chocolate Nut Clusters	50
101.	Cocoa Coconut Butter Fat Bombs	51

102.	Blueberry Lemon Cake	51
103.	Rich Chocolate Mousse	51
104.	Home Made Coconut Ice Cream	52
105.	Berries with Coconut Cream	52
106.	Coconut Panna Cotta	52
107.	Lemon & Lime Sorbet	53
108.	Avocado Kale Keto Bowl	53
109.	Mozzarella Sticks	53
110.	Avocado Taco Boats	54
111.	Cheesy Biscuits	54

30-DAY MEAL PLAN 56

CONCLUSION 63

INTRODUCTION

Diets are often met with criticism, and the keto diet is not immune to controversy. In particular, some have raised concerns about the high fat intake that keto requires, as fatty foods are known to raise cholesterol and cause heart disease. However, studies had shown that low-carb regimens win out against all others when carefully planned and adhered to. They are not only advantageous to those trying to lose weight but come with a whole host of extra health benefits that will improve your overall well-being. In some cases, the keto diet can even reduce your cholesterol levels. Let's delve deeper into the various perks of the keto diet. The primary process at play with the ketogenic diet is ketosis. Entering this metabolic state has been shown to positively impact the body in several ways, even if you are only on a diet for a brief period. Ketosis itself has some benefits. It has been shown to:

- It improves the body's ability to draw on fats as an energy source.
- Spare your proteins, as your body starts to use ketones as fuel instead.
- Lower insulin levels in the body that influences the secretion of growth hormones.

Now let's get to grips with some of the overall benefits of the ketogenic diet.

Suppressed appetite – Most diets require you to reduce your overall food consumption, and the consequential hunger is likely to cause you some discomfort. Hunger is a stumbling block for many, and a notable reason why so many dieters fail. Low-carb diets, on the other hand, have the added benefit of reducing your appetite. Cutting carbs and substituting them with fats and proteins means you cut your caloric intake without going hungry.

Increased potential for weight loss – Compared with many other popular diets, low-carb regimens promote a much faster weight loss rate. Low carbohydrates help reduce the excess water in the body, which often accounts for a considerable percentage of our unwanted pounds. Moreover, the keto diet diminishes insulin levels, flushing the body of the surplus sodium that retains the extra weight.

Reduction of triglycerides – The presence of triglycerides, or fat molecules, in the body correlates strongly with illnesses like heart disease. The fewer carbs you consume, the fewer triglycerides there are in your system, which is excellent news for your long-term health.

More good cholesterol – You may be under the impression that cholesterol is universally bad for you. Still, there is, in fact, a form of cholesterol that reduces the risk of heart disease: high-density lipoprotein or HDL. The increased consumption of fats associated with the keto diet raises levels of HDL. HDL is not only a positive addition to your system, but it helps eradicate lousy cholesterol (LDL) from your bloodstream.

Reduced blood sugar and insulin levels – Carbohydrate-rich foods are broken down into simple sugars by our digestive system, which inevitably elevates blood sugar levels. Insulin is needed to combat these toxins. A high-carb diet, maintained over a long period, can interfere with the body's ability to produce insulin, leading to type 2 diabetes. The ketogenic diet is advantageous in this regard, as it lowers blood sugar and insulin levels significantly.

Natural cancer treatment – According to some researchers, disciplined regulation of your body's metabolic functions can potentially reduce the risk of and even treat cancer. Low-carb diets deprive cancerous cells of fuel, as these types of cells feed off of glucose and cannot adapt to the shift in energy sources involved with ketosis. As a result, the keto diet may be able to prevent cancerous cells from spreading.

Treatment for metabolic syndrome – Metabolic syndrome is a severe medical condition that increases the risk of heart disease, diabetes, and stroke. There are numerous symptoms, including:

- Low levels of HDL
- High triglyceride levels
- Raised fasting blood sugar levels
- Elevated blood pressure

Therapy for some brain disorders – Certain parts of our brains relies exclusively on glucose for fuel. That is why our livers need to derive glucose from protein if our carb intake is low. However, larger sections of the brain are capable of using ketones for fuel. With the keto diet, specific biochemical changes may occur in the mind, potentially eradicating the circuit system responsible for seizures. Think back to Hugh Conklin and his use of the ketogenic diet to treat sufferers of epileptic seizures – 50% of his patients reported their condition was much improved.

BREAKFAST

1. Peanut Butter Cup Smoothie

Preparation Time: 5 minutes

Cooking Time: 0 minute

Servings: 2

INGREDIENTS:

- 1 cup of water
- ¾ cup coconut cream
- 1 scoop chocolate protein powder
- 2 tablespoons natural peanut butter
- 3 ice cubes

DIRECTIONS:

1. Put the water, coconut cream, protein powder, peanut butter, and ice in a blender and blend until smooth.
2. Pour into 2 glasses and serve immediately.

NUTRITION: Calories: 486 Cal Fat: 40g Carbs: 11g Protein: 30g Fiber: 5g

2. Berry Green Smoothie

Preparation Time: 10 minutes

Cooking Time: 0 minute

Servings: 2

INGREDIENTS:

- 1 cup of water
- ½ cup raspberries
- ½ cup shredded kale
- ¾ cup cream cheese
- 1 tablespoon coconut oil
- 1 scoop vanilla protein powder

DIRECTIONS:

1. Blend all the ingredients until smooth.
2. Pour into 2 glasses and serve immediately.

NUTRITION: Calories: 436 cal Fat: 36g Carbs: 11g Protein: 28g Fiber: 5g

3. Lemon-Cashew Smoothie

Preparation Time: 5 minutes

Cooking Time: 0 minute

Servings: 1

INGREDIENTS:

- 1 cup unsweetened cashew milk
- ¼ cup heavy (whipping) cream
- ¼ cup freshly squeezed lemon juice
- 1 scoop plain protein powder
- 1 tablespoon coconut oil
- 1 teaspoon sweetener

DIRECTIONS:

1. Put the cashew milk, heavy cream, lemon juice, protein powder, coconut oil, and sweetener in a blender and blend until smooth.
2. Pour into a glass and serve immediately.

NUTRITION: Calories: 503 cal Fat: 45g Carbs: 15g Protein: 29g Fiber: 4g

4. Spinach-Blueberry Smoothie

Preparation Time: 5 minutes

Cooking Time: 0 minute

Servings: 2

INGREDIENTS:

- 1 cup of coconut milk
- 1 cup spinach
- ½ English cucumber, chopped
- ½ cup blueberries
- 1 scoop plain protein powder
- 2 tablespoons coconut oil
- 4 ice cubes
- Mint sprigs, for garnish

DIRECTIONS:

1. Put the coconut milk, spinach, cucumber, blueberries, protein powder, coconut oil, and ice in a blender and blend until smooth.
2. Pour into 2 glasses, garnish each with the mint, and serve immediately.

NUTRITION: Calories: 353 cal Fat: 32g Carbs: 9g Protein: 15g Fiber: 3g

5. <u>Creamy Cinnamon Smoothie</u>

Preparation Time: 5 minutes

Cooking Time: 0 minute

Servings: 2

INGREDIENTS:

- 2 cups of coconut milk
- 1 scoop vanilla protein powder
- 5 drops liquid stevia
- 1 teaspoon ground cinnamon
- ½ teaspoon alcohol-free vanilla extract

DIRECTIONS:

1. Put the coconut milk, protein powder, stevia, cinnamon, and vanilla in a blender and blend until smooth.
2. Pour into 2 glasses and serve immediately.

NUTRITION: Calories: 492 cal Fat: 47g Carbs: 8g Protein: 18g Fiber: 2g

6. <u>Nut Medley Granola</u>

Preparation Time: 10 minutes

Cooking Time: 1 hour

Servings: 8

INGREDIENTS:

- 2 cups shredded unsweetened coconut
- 1 cup sliced almonds
- 1 cup raw sunflower seeds
- ½ cup raw pumpkin seeds
- ½ cup walnuts
- ½ cup melted coconut oil

- 10 drops liquid stevia
- 1 teaspoon ground cinnamon
- ½ teaspoon ground nutmeg

DIRECTIONS:

1. Preheat the oven to 250°F. Line 2 baking sheets with parchment paper. Set aside.
2. Put together the shredded coconut, almonds, sunflower seeds, pumpkin seeds, and walnuts in a large bowl until mixed.
3. Blend together the coconut oil, stevia, cinnamon, and nutmeg until blended.
4. Combine the coconut oil mixture and nut mixture. Utilize your hands to mix together until the nuts are very well coated.
5. Place the granola mixture on the baking sheets and spread it out evenly.
6. Bake the granola, stir every 10 minutes, until the mixture is golden brown and crunchy, about 1 hour.
7. Move the granola to a large bowl and let the granola cool, tossing it frequently to break up the large pieces.
8. Keep the granola inside airtight containers in the refrigerator or freezer for up to 1 month.

NUTRITION: Calories: 391 cal Fat: 38g Carbs: 10g Protein: 10g Fiber: 6g

7. <u>Bacon-Artichoke Omelet</u>

Preparation Time: 10 minutes

Cooking Time: 10 minutes

Servings: 4

INGREDIENTS:

- 6 eggs, beaten
- 2 tablespoons heavy (whipping) cream
- 8 bacon slices, cooked and chopped
- 1 tablespoon olive oil
- ¼ cup chopped onion
- ½ cup chopped artichoke hearts (canned, packed in water)
- Sea salt

- Freshly ground black pepper

DIRECTIONS:

1. Beat together the eggs, heavy cream, and bacon until well blended, and set aside.
2. Get a huge skillet, place it over medium-high heat and add the olive oil.
3. Sauté the onion until tender, about 3 minutes.
4. Pour the egg mixture into the skillet, swirling it for 1 minute.
5. Cook the omelet on both sides for 2 minutes.
6. Sprinkle the artichoke hearts on top and flip the omelet. Cook for 4 minutes more until the egg is firm. Flip the omelet over again, so the artichoke hearts are on top.
7. Remove from the heat, cut the omelet into quarters, and season with salt and black pepper. Transfer the omelet to plates and serve.

NUTRITION: Calories: 435 cal Fat: 39g Carbs: 5g Protein: 17g Fiber: 2g

8. Mushroom Frittata

Preparation Time: 10 minutes

Cooking Time: 5 minutes

Servings: 6

INGREDIENTS:

- 2 tablespoons olive oil
- 1 cup sliced fresh mushrooms
- 1 cup shredded spinach
- 6 bacon slices, cooked and chopped
- 10 large eggs, beaten
- ½ cup crumbled goat cheese
- Sea salt
- Freshly ground black pepper

DIRECTIONS:

1. Preheat the oven to 350°F.
2. Put an ovenproof skillet and add the olive oil.

3. Fry the mushrooms until they turn lightly brown, about 3 minutes.
4. Add the bacon and spinach then sauté until the greens are wilted about a minute.
5. Add the eggs and cook, lifting the edges of the frittata with a spatula so uncooked egg flows underneath, for 3 to 4 minutes.
6. Season lightly with salt and pepper.
7. Bake until lightly browned, about 15 minutes.
8. Take away the frittata from the oven, and let it stand for 5 minutes.
9. Cut into 6 wedges and serve immediately.

NUTRITION: Calories: 316 cal Fat: 27g Carbs: 1g Protein: 16g Fiber: 0g

9. Breakfast Bake

Preparation Time: 10 minutes

Cooking Time: 50 minutes

Servings: 8

INGREDIENTS:

- 1 tbsp olive oil
- 1 pound preservative-free or homemade sausage
- 8 large eggs
- 2 cups cooked spaghetti squash
- 1 tablespoon chopped fresh oregano
- Sea salt
- Freshly ground black pepper
- ½ cup shredded Cheddar cheese

DIRECTIONS:

1. Preheat the oven to 375°F. Put an olive oil into a 9-by-13-inch casserole dish and set aside.
2. Place a huge ovenproof skillet over medium-high heat and add the olive oil.
3. Brown the sausage until cooked through, about 5 minutes. While the sausage is cooking, whisk together the eggs, squash, and oregano in a medium bowl. Put a little salt and pepper and set aside.

4. Add the cooked sausage to the egg mixture, stir until just combined, and pour the mixture into the casserole dish.

5. Dust the top of the casserole with the cheese and cover the casserole loosely with aluminum foil.

6. Bake the casserole for 30 minutes, and then take away the foil and bake for another 15 minutes.

7. Allow it to cool for 15 minutes before serving.

NUTRITION: Calories: 303 cal Fat: 24g Carbs: 4g Protein: 17g Fiber: 1g

10. Avocado And Eggs

Preparation Time: 10 minutes

Cooking Time: 20 minutes

Servings: 4

INGREDIENTS:

- 2 avocados, peeled, halved lengthwise, and pitted
- 4 large eggs
- 1 (4-ounce) chicken breast, cooked and shredded
- ¼ cup Cheddar cheese
- Sea salt
- Freshly ground black pepper

DIRECTIONS:

1. Preheat the oven to 420°F

2. Get a spoon and empty out each side of the avocado halves until the hole is about twice the original size.

3. Place the avocado halves in an 8-by-8-inch baking dish, hollow side up.

4. Crack an egg into each hollow and divide the shredded chicken between each avocado half. Put a a a cheese on top of each and season lightly with the salt and pepper.

5. Bake the avocados until the eggs are cooked through, about 15 to 20 minutes.

6. Serve immediately.

NUTRITION: Calories: 324 cal Fat: 25g Carbs: 8g Protein: 19g Fiber: 5g

MAINS

11. Verde Chicken Enchiladas

Preparation Time: 20 minutes

Cooking Time: 20 minutes

Servings: 8

INGREDIENTS:

- 2 (4.2-ounce) boneless, skinless chicken breasts, cooked
- ½ cup cooked, diced mushrooms
- ½ cup cooked, diced zucchini
- 8 small low-carb flour tortillas
- 1 cup green enchilada sauce
- 1 cup shredded Cheddar cheese
- 1 medium green onion, finely chopped
- ¼ cup freshly minced cilantro, divided
- ¼ cup sliced black olives
- ⅓ cup full-fat sour cream

DIRECTIONS:

1. Preheat oven to 350°F. Grease a 9" × 9" baking dish.
2. In a medium bowl, finely shred cooked chicken breasts. Put in mushrooms and zucchini and blend well.
3. On a large baking sheet or clean cutting board, lay out tortillas one at a time and evenly distribute chicken and vegetable mixture in the center of each tortilla. Roll each tortilla over chicken and vegetables to make tight rolls.
4. Put rolls in baking dish. Cover with green enchilada sauce and evenly top with cheese, green onion, half of the cilantro, and olives.
5. Bake 15–20 minutes until cheese melts.
6. Let cool 10 minutes. Top with sour cream and remaining cilantro and serve.

NUTRITION: Calories: 200 Fat: 10g Carbs:18g Protein: 15g

12. "K.F.C." Keto Fried Chicken

Preparation Time: 15 minutes

Cooking Time: 10 minutes

Servings: 4

INGREDIENTS:

- 1 cup vegetable oil, for frying
- 2 large eggs
- 2 tablespoons heavy whipping cream
- ⅔ cup blanched almond flour
- ⅔ cup grated Parmesan cheese
- ¼ tsp salt
- ½ tsp black pepper
- ½ tsp paprika
- ½ tsp ground cayenne
- 4 boneless, skinless chicken thighs

DIRECTIONS:

1. In a medium-sized pot over average heat, add vegetable oil. Make sure it is about an inch deep. Heat oil to 360°F.
2. In a bowl, add eggs and whipping cream. Blend until well mixed.
3. In a separate bowl, add salt, pepper, paprika, almond flour, Parmesan cheese,and cayenne and mix.
4. Cut each thigh into 2. If wet, tap dry.
5. Coat 2 piece in the dry breading first, then in the egg wash, and then the breading again.
6. Shake to get rud of any excess breading and lower the chicken into the hot oil. Cook until deep brown or for about 3–5 minutes on each side, and then drain on paper towels.
7. Repeat until every chicken is cooked. Serve right away while hot and crispy.

NUTRITION: Calories: 470 Fat: 34g Carbs: 5g Protein: 31g

13. <u>Turkey Taco Boats</u>

Preparation Time: 10 minutes

Cooking Time: 30 minutes

Servings: 4

INGREDIENTS:

- 1 pound lean ground turkey
- 1 (1-ounce) package taco seasoning
- ¾ cup of water
- ½ small onion, peeled and finely chopped
- ½ large green bell pepper, seeded and chopped
- 1 (4-ounce) can tomato sauce
- 8 large romaine lettuce leaves
- 1 small tomato, diced

DIRECTIONS:

1. In a medium-sized pan over average heat, brown turkey. (There shouldn't be any fat to drain.) Stir in seasoning packet and water.
2. Add bell pepper, onion, and tomato sauce to meat and stir. Cover and reduce heat to low for 15 minutes.
3. Add two lettuce "boats" per plate and fill one-eighth of the meat mixture into each boat.
4. Top with fresh tomato and serve.

NUTRITION: Calories: 220 Fat: 9g Carbs: 10g Protein: 23g

14. <u>Alex's "Chick And Brock" Casserole</u>

Preparation Time: 10 minutes

Cooking Time: 50 minutes

Servings: 8

INGREDIENTS:

- 1 cup heavy whipping cream

- 1 cup mascarpone cheese, softened
- 1 cup grated Parmesan cheese
- 3 cloves garlic, peeled and minced
- 2 teaspoons dried parsley
- ½ teaspoon salt
- ½ teaspoon black pepper
- ½ teaspoon garlic salt
- 1 pound cooked, shredded boneless chicken breast
- 4 cups raw broccoli florets
- 2 cups of shredded mozzarella cheese

DIRECTIONS:

1. Preheat oven to 375°F. Grease a 9" × 12" casserole dish.
2. In a huge bowl, put all ingredients except chicken, broccoli, and mozzarella. Mix until blended to a thick sauce.
3. In a separate large bowl, mix shredded chicken, broccoli, and 1 cup mozzarella. Add sauce mixture and mix well.
4. Transfer to the casserole dish. Spread remaining 1 cup mozzarella evenly over the top.
5. Bake, 40–50 minutes or until broccoli, is tender and cheese is golden brown.

NUTRITION: Calories: 427 Fat: 23g Carbs: 9g Protein: 31g

15. <u>Stuffed Chicken For Suppah</u>

Preparation Time: 10 minutes

Cooking Time: 24 minutes

Servings: 4

INGREDIENTS:

- 6 ounces chopped fresh spinach
- 2 cloves garlic, peeled and minced
- 1½ cups crumbled feta cheese, divided
- 2 ounces full-fat cream cheese, softened
- 4 (4.8-ounce) boneless, skinless chicken breasts

- ¼ tsp black pepper
- 2 tomatoes, each sliced into 8 rounds

DIRECTIONS:

1. Preheat oven to 440°F. Arrange the baking sheet with greased foil.
2. Cook spinach in a skillet 4–5 minutes over medium heat. Let it cool, then press out extra moisture.
3. To a bowl, put spinach, garlic, and ¾ cup of feta cheese.
4. Put the cream cheese into the microwave and let it soft for 15–30 seconds.
5. Add to spinach mixture, stirring thoroughly.
6. Place chicken on a baking sheet. Cut a horizontal slit in every breast, creating a pocket.
7. Fill each breast with a quarter of the spinach mixture. Sprinkle with pepper.
8. Put four tomato slices and remaining feta.on top of the chicken breast.
9. Bake for 16–20 minutes or until the chicken is thoroughly cooked.
10. Tent pan with foil if the cheese starts to brown before the chicken is done.

NUTRITION: Calories: 364 Fat: 19g Carbs: 7g Protein: 40g

16. **Silky Chicken With Mushroom Sauce**

Preparation Time: 10 minutes

Cooking Time: 20 minutes

Servings: 4

INGREDIENTS:

- 4 (4.2-ounce) boneless, skinless chicken breasts
- 4 tablespoons olive oil, divided
- 2 cups sliced mushrooms
- ½ cup diced onion
- 2 tablespoons unblanched almond flour

- 1 clove garlic, peeled and minced
- ½ cup half and half, divided
- 2 tablespoons chopped dried thyme
- ¼ teaspoon salt
- ¼ teaspoon black pepper

DIRECTIONS:

1. Pound chicken breasts to even thickness, about ¼" thick.
2. In a large sauté pan over medium heat, heat 2 tablespoons olive oil and then add chicken. Cook 1–2 minutes until brown on each side. Reduce heat to low.
3. Cover with a secure lid and let cook an additional 15 minutes (flipping at 7½ minutes). After 10 minutes, remove chicken from pan, and cover to keep warm.
4. In the same pan, add mushrooms, 2 tablespoons oil, and onion. Cook over medium heat 10–15 minutes, stirring regularly. Stir in almond flour to thicken and cook an additional 2–3 minutes.
5. Add garlic, ¼ cup half and half, thyme, salt, and pepper. Keep stirring, adding more half and a half if needed until the desired consistency is achieved.
6. Serve warm chicken on a plate topped with mushroom sauce.

NUTRITION: Calories: Fat: 20g Carbs: 7g Protein: 29g

17. **Indoor Bbq Chicken**

Preparation Time: 10 minutes

Cooking Time: 45 minutes

Servings: 4

INGREDIENTS:

- 1 tablespoon sriracha sauce
- 2 teaspoons chili powder
- 2 teaspoons garlic powder
- 2 teaspoons onion powder
- 1 teaspoon salt

- 1 teaspoon black pepper
- 1 tablespoon apple cider vinegar
- 1 tablespoon paprika
- 1 (1-gram) packet 0g net carb sweetener
- ½ teaspoon xanthan gum
- 1 cup crushed tomatoes
- 4 medium chicken thighs with skin

DIRECTIONS:

1. Preheat oven to 375°F. Arrange the baking sheet with greased foil.
2. Over medium heat, make the barbecue sauce by mixing all the ingredients except the chicken and bring to boil. Let simmer 5 minutes, stirring regularly.
3. Using a basting brush, apply about half the barbecue sauce to both sides of the thighs—place chicken on a baking sheet.
4. Cook 20 minutes. Flip chicken and reapply remaining sauce. Cook another 20 minutes until chicken is thoroughly cooked.
5. Serve warm or cold.

NUTRITION: Calories: 362 Fat: 19g Carbs: 10g Protein: 34g

18. Chipotle Chicken Fajita Bowl

Preparation Time: 10 minutes

Cooking Time: 30 minutes

Servings: 4

INGREDIENTS:

- 3 tablespoons unsalted butter
- 1½ pounds boneless and skinless chicken thighs, sliced into thin strips
- ¼ teaspoon salt
- 1 yellow onion
- 1 green bell pepper
- 2 tablespoons taco seasoning
- 6 cups chopped romaine lettuce
- 1 cup shredded Mexican cheese
- ½ cup full-fat sour cream

- 2 large avocados, peeled, pitted, and diced
- 1 small tomato, chopped
- 4 tablespoons finely chopped cilantro

DIRECTIONS:

1. To start, add butter and fry chicken in a large skillet for 5 minutes while stirring just to brown. Season chicken with salt. Sauté 10–15 minutes, stirring regularly.
2. Add onion, bell pepper, and taco seasoning. Decrease heat to low and cook 8–10 minutes. Stir often until vegetables have softened.
3. Distribute lettuce evenly to serving bowls, then add cooked chicken and vegetables. Top with cheese, sour cream, diced avocados, tomato, and cilantro.

NUTRITION: Calories: 610 Fat: 40g Carbs: 16g Protein: 39g

19. Fluffy Chicken

Preparation Time: 3 hours

Cooking Time: 5 hours and 30 minutes

Servings: 8

INGREDIENTS:

- ½ cup chicken broth
- 1 (1-ounce) package ranch powder seasoning mix
- 2 pounds boneless, skinless chicken breasts
- 8 ounces full-fat cream cheese, softened
- 8 slices no-sugar-added bacon, cooked and crumbled
- ½ cup shredded Cheddar cheese

DIRECTIONS:

1. Add chicken broth to slow cooker and stir in ranch powder seasoning packet.
2. Add chicken and cover—Cook 2 hours 45 minutes on high or 5 hours 15 minutes on low.

3. Remove lid. Drain excess broth, leaving around ½ cup for moisture depending on preference.
4. Shred chicken.
5. In a microwave-safe bowl, microwave the cream cheese for 20–30 seconds. Combine with crumbled bacon and Cheddar cheese.
6. 6 Add cream cheese mixture to shredded chicken. Cover and heat 10 minutes on high temperature until cheeses melt. Serve warm.

NUTRITION: Calories: 325 Fat: 16g Carbs: 3g Protein: 33g

20. N'awlins Chicken

Preparation Time: minutes

Cooking Time: minutes

Servings: 6

INGREDIENTS:

- 1 teaspoon olive oil
- 2 pounds boneless, skinless chicken thighs
- ¼ teaspoon salt
- ⅛ teaspoon black pepper
- 3 tablespoons unsalted butter
- ¼ cup minced onion
- 3 cloves garlic, peeled and minced
- 1 cup bourbon
- 2 cups chicken stock

DIRECTIONS:

1. Put in olive oil in a saucepan, then add chicken thighs. Season with salt and pepper and sear 3 minutes on each side until golden brown.
2. Add butter, onion, and garlic, and sauté until the onion and garlic are brown (3–5 minutes).
3. Pour bourbon and chicken stock over chicken and boil.
4. Reduce heat to medium and cook 25–30 minutes, flipping chicken halfway through.

5. Cool and serve the chicken with bourbon sauce.

NUTRITION: Calories: 391 Fat: 18g Carbs: 4g Protein: 40g

21. Four Horsemen Butter Chicken

Preparation Time: 10 minutes

Cooking Time: 27 minutes

Servings: 8

INGREDIENTS:

- 1 tablespoon unsalted butter
- 1 tablespoon olive oil
- 1 medium onion, peeled and diced
- 3 cloves garlic, peeled and minced
- 2 teaspoons peeled and grated fresh ginger
- 2 pounds skinless chicken breasts, cooked and cut into ¾" chunks
- 3 ounces tomato paste
- 3 ounces red curry paste
- 1 tablespoon garam masala
- 1 teaspoon chili powder
- 1 teaspoon mustard seeds
- 1 teaspoon ground coriander
- 1 teaspoon curry
- 1 teaspoon salt
- ⅛ teaspoon black pepper
- 1 (14-ounce) can of unsweetened coconut milk
- 1 teaspoon chopped cilantro

DIRECTIONS:

1. Put in butter in a large pan over medium heat, and add olive oil. Add onion and fry until soft, about 3–5 minutes. Mix in garlic and ginger. Cook 1–2 minutes more.
2. Add cooked chicken to skillet. Add tomato paste, red curry paste, garam masala, chili powder, mustard seeds, coriander, and

curry. Add salt and pepper. Stir until well mixed, and chicken cubes are well coated.

3. Blend in coconut milk and bring to boil. Reduce heat. Cover and simmer 20 minutes.

4. Remove from heat. Cool for 10 minutes and serve warm with cilantro sprinkled on top.

NUTRITION: Calories: 298 Fat: 16g Carbs: 8g Protein: 30g

SIDES

22. Cheesy Bacon & Eggplant Gratin

Preparation Time: 10 minutes

Cooking Time: 40 minutes

Servings: 4

INGREDIENTS:

- 6 bacon slices, chopped
- 3 large eggplants, sliced
- 1 tbsp dried oregano
- 2 tbsp chopped parsley
- Salt and black pepper to taste
- ½ cup crumbled feta cheese
- ¾ cup heavy cream
- ½ cup shredded Parmesan

DIRECTIONS:

1. Preheat your oven to 400 F. Put bacon in a skillet and fry over medium heat until brown and crispy, 6 minutes; transfer to a plate.
2. Arrange half of the eggplants in a greased baking sheet and season with oregano, parsley, salt, and pepper.
3. Scatter half of bacon and half of feta cheese on top and repeat the layering process using the remaining ingredients.
4. In a bowl, combine heavy cream with half of the Parmesan cheese, and spread on top of the layered ingredients. Sprinkle with the remaining Parmesan.
5. Bake until the cream is bubbly and the gratin golden, 20 minutes. Serve.

NUTRITION: Calories: 433 Fat: 29g Carbs: 1.7g Protein: 16g

23. Wrapped Halloumi in Bacon

Preparation Time: 10 minutes

Cooking Time: 20 minutes

Servings: 4

INGREDIENTS:

- ½ lb halloumi cheese, cut into 16 cubes
- 16 bacon strips
- ½ cup swerve brown sugar
- ½ cup mayonnaise
- ¼ cup hot sauce

DIRECTIONS:

1. Lay bacon in a skillet and cook over medium heat on both sides until crisp, 5 minutes; transfer to a plate.
2. Wrap each halloumi cheese with a bacon strip and secure with a toothpick each. Place on a baking sheet.
3. In a bowl, combine swerve brown sugar, mayonnaise, and hot sauce.
4. Pour the mixture all over the bacon-halloumi pieces and bake in the oven at 350 F for 10 minutes. Serve chilled.

NUTRITION: Calories: 346 Fat: 25 g Carbs: 4.6 g Protein: 13 g

24. Sweet Mustard Mini Sausages

Preparation Time: 5 minutes

Cooking Time: 10 minutes

Servings: 4

INGREDIENTS:

- 1 cup swerve brown sugar
- 3 tbsp almond flour
- 2 tsp mustard powder
- ¼ cup lemon juice
- ¼ cup white wine vinegar
- 1 tsp tamari sauce
- 2 lb mini smoked sausages

DIRECTIONS:

1. In a pot, combine swerve brown sugar, almond flour, and mustard.
2. Gradually stir in lemon juice, vinegar, and tamari sauce. Bring to a boil over medium heat while stirring until thickened, 2 minutes.
3. Mix in sausages until adequately coated. Cook them for 5 minutes. Serve warm.

NUTRITION: Calories: 2744 Fat: 45 g Carbs: 7 g Protein: 24 g

25. Chili Broccoli & Pancetta Roast

Preparation Time: 10 minutes

Cooking Time: 30 minutes

Servings: 4

INGREDIENTS:

- 1 lb broccoli rabe, halved
- 6 pancetta slices, chopped
- 2 tbsp olive oil
- ¼ tsp red chili flakes

DIRECTIONS:

1. Preheat oven to 425 F. Place broccoli rabe in a greased baking sheet and top with pancetta.
2. Drizzle with olive oil, season to taste, and sprinkle with chili flakes.
3. Roast for 30 minutes. Serve warm and enjoy!

NUTRITION : Calories: 125Fat: 10 g Carbs: 0.2 g Protein: 7 g

26. Chili Turnip Fries

Preparation Time: 10 minutes

Cooking Time: 40 minutes

Servings: 4

INGREDIENTS:

- 4 large parsnips, sliced
- 3 tbsp ground pork rinds

- 3 tbsp olive oil
- ¼ tsp red chili flakes

DIRECTIONS:

1. Preheat oven to 425 F. Pour parsnips into a bowl and add in the pork rinds.
2. Toss and place the parsnips on a baking sheet. Drizzle with olive oil and sprinkle with chili flakes.
3. Bake until crispy, 40-45 minutes, tossing halfway. Serve.

NUTRITION: Calories: 260 Fat: 11 g Carbs: 22.6 g Protein: 3 g

27. Buttery Radish & Minute Steak Sauté

Preparation Time: 5 minutes

Cooking Time: 25 minutes

Servings: 4

INGREDIENTS:

- 10 oz minute steak, cut into small pieces
- 3 tbsp butter
- 1½ lb radishes, quartered
- 1 garlic clove, minced
- 2 tbsp freshly chopped thyme

DIRECTIONS:

1. Place the butter in a skillet and melt it over medium heat, season the meat with salt and pepper, and brown it until brown on all sides, 12 minutes; transfer to a plate.
2. Add and sauté radishes, garlic, and thyme until the radishes are cooked, 10 minutes.
3. Plate and serve warm.

NUTRITION: Calories: 252 Fat: 16g Carbs: 0.4g Protein: 21g

28. Cheddar Bacon & Celeriac Bake

Preparation Time: 10 minutes

Cooking Time: 40 minutes

Servings: 4

INGREDIENTS:

- 6 bacon slices, chopped
- 3 tbsp butter
- 3 garlic cloves, minced
- 3 tbsp almond flour
- 2 cups coconut cream
- 1 cup chicken broth
- Salt and black pepper to taste
- 1 lb celeriac, peeled and sliced
- 2 cups shredded cheddar
- ¼ cup chopped scallions

DIRECTIONS:

1. Preheat your oven to 400 F. Add bacon to a skillet and fry over medium heat until brown and crispy.
2. Spoon onto a plate. Melt butter in the same skillet and sauté garlic for 1 minute.
3. Mix in almond flour and cook for another minute. Whisk in coconut cream, chicken broth, salt, and pepper. Simmer for 5 minutes.
4. Spread a layer of the sauce in a greased casserole dish and arrange layer celeriac on top.
5. Cover with more sauce, top with some bacon and cheddar cheese, and scatter scallions on top. Repeat the layering procedure until all the ingredients are exhausted.
6. Bake for 35 minutes. Let it rest for a few minutes and serve.

NUTRITION: Calories: 981 Fat: 86 g Carbs: 20 g Protein: 28 g

29. Easy Bacon & Cheese Balls

Preparation Time: 10 minutes

Cooking Time: 5 minutes

Servings: 4

INGREDIENTS:

- 7 bacon slices
- 6 oz cream cheese
- 6 oz shredded Gruyere cheese
- 2 tbsp butter, softened
- ½ tsp red chili flakes

DIRECTIONS:

1. Put bacon in a skillet and fry over medium heat until crispy, 5 minutes.
2. Transfer to a plate to cool and crumble it. Put the bacon grease inside a bowl and mix in cream cheese, Gruyere cheese, butter, and red chili flakes.
3. Refrigerate to set for 15 minutes.
4. Remove and mold into walnut-sized balls. Roll in the crumbled bacon. Plate and serve.

NUTRITION: Calories: 538 Fat: 50g Carbs: 0.5g Protein: 22g

SEAFOOD

30. Cheesy Tuna Pâté

Preparation Time: 10 minutes

Cooking Time: 0 minutes

Servings: 6

INGREDIENTS:

- 2 (6-ounce) cans tuna in oil, drained
- 1 tablespoon fresh Italian parsley, chopped
- 1/2 cup Cottage cheese
- 1-ounce sunflower seeds, ground
- 1-ounce sesame seeds, ground
- 1/2 teaspoon mustard seeds

DIRECTIONS:

1. Put all the indgredients in your blender or food processor.
2. Blend until everything is well combined.

NUTRITION: Calories: 181 Fat: 10.4g Carbs: 2.1g Protein: 19g

31. Cheesy Salmon Dip

Preparation Time: 5 minutes

Cooking Time: 10 minutes

Servings: 10

INGREDIENTS:

- 10 ounces salmon
- 4 hard-boiled egg yolks, finely chopped
- 1/4 cup fresh scallions, chopped
- 5 ounces Ricotta cheese
- 5 ounces full-fat cream cheese
- Salt and freshly ground black pepper, to your liking
- 1/2 teaspoon hot paprika

DIRECTIONS:

1. Grill the salmon for about 10 minutes until browned and flakes easily with a fork. Cut into small chunks.

2. Mix all of the mentioned ingredients until they become well incorporated.

NUTRITION: Calories: 109 Fat: 6.3g Carbs: 1.3g Protein: 11.4g

32. Easy Halibut Steaks

Preparation Time: 30 minutes

Cooking Time: 15 minutes

Servings: 2

INGREDIENTS:

- 2 halibut steaks
- 1 teaspoon garlic, finely minced
- 1/3 cup freshly squeezed lime juice
- 1 teaspoon dry rosemary
- 1 teaspoon dry thyme
- 4 tablespoons fresh chives, chopped
- 2 teaspoons sesame oil, room temperature
- Flaky sea salt and white pepper, to taste

DIRECTIONS:

1. Place the fresh lime juice, sesame oil, salt, white pepper, rosemary, thyme, chives, garlic, and halibut steak in a ceramic dish; let it marinate for about 30 minutes.
2. Grill the halibut steaks approximately 15 minutes, turning occasionally and basting with the reserved marinade.

NUTRITION: Calories: 308 Fat: 10.9g Carbs: 2g Protein: 46.5g

33. Cholula Shrimp Spread

Preparation Time: 10 minutes

Cooking Time: 0 minutes

Servings: 8

INGREDIENTS:

- 12 ounces shrimp, canned and drained
- 1 tablespoon Cholula
- 1/2 cup mayonnaise

- 2 teaspoons green garlic, finely minced
- Sea salt and ground black pepper
- 1 teaspoon cayenne pepper
- 1/2 teaspoon dried rosemary

DIRECTIONS:

1. In a mixing bowl, put and mix all of the ingredients until well incorporated.
2. Cover and transfer to your refrigerator until thoroughly chilled.

NUTRITION: Calories: 108 Fat: 5.4g Carbs: 5g Protein: 8.2g

34. **Sherry and Butter Prawns**

Preparation Time: 1 hour

Cooking Time: 10 minutes

Servings: 4

INGREDIENTS:

- 1 ½ pounds king prawns, peeled and deveined
- 2 tablespoons dry sherry
- 1 teaspoon dried basil
- 1/2 teaspoon mustard seeds
- 1 ½ tablespoon fresh lemon juice
- 1 teaspoon cayenne pepper, crushed
- 1 tablespoon garlic paste
- 1/2 stick butter, at room temperature

DIRECTIONS:

1. Whisk the dry sherry with cayenne pepper, garlic paste, basil, mustard seeds, lemon juice, and prawns. Let it marinate for 1 hour in your refrigerator.
2. In a frying pan, melt the butter over medium-high flame, basting with the reserved marinade.

NUTRITION: Calories: 29   Fat: 14.3g Carbs: 3.6g Protein: 34.6g

35. **Super Easy Fish Cakes**

Preparation Time: 5 minutes

Cooking Time: 25 minutes

Servings: 6

INGREDIENTS:

- 1 ½ pound tilapia fish, deboned and flaked
- 2 tablespoons sesame oil
- 1/2 cup of Cottage cheese, at room temperature
- 2 eggs, lightly beaten
- 1/4 cup almond meal
- 1/4 tablespoons flax meal
- 2 teaspoons brown mustard
- Sea salt and pepper, to taste
- 2 tablespoons fresh basil, chopped

DIRECTIONS:

1. Mix the flaked fish with the eggs, almond and flax meal, cheese, mustard, salt, pepper, and basil. Form the mixture into 12 patties.
2. Now, place the patties on a parchment-lined baking sheet. Spritz them with sesame oil.
3. Bake in the preheated oven at 395 degrees F for approximately 25 minutes, rotating the pan occasionally once.

NUTRITION: Calories: 234 Fat: 10.6g Carbs: 2.5g Protein: 31.2g

36. **Zingy Tuna Steaks with Spinach**

Preparation Time: 10 minutes

Cooking Time: 10 minutes

Servings: 6

INGREDIENTS:

- 2 pounds tuna steaks
- 3 cups spinach
- 1 tablespoon Dijon mustard
- 3 tablespoons peanut oil
- Salt and pepper, to season

- 1/2 cup radishes, thinly sliced
- 1 fresh lemon, sliced
- 1 cup green onions, thinly sliced

DIRECTIONS:

1. Brush each tuna steaks with peanut oil and season them with salt and pepper.
2. Arrange the tuna steaks on a foil-lined baking pan. Top with lemon slices, cover with foil, and roast at 400 degrees F for about 10 minutes.

NUTRITION: Calories: 444 Fat: 38.2g Carbs: 4.7g Protein: 21.9g

37. Clams with Garlic-Tomato Sauce

Preparation Time: minutes

Cooking Time: minutes

Servings: 4

INGREDIENTS:

- 40 littleneck clams
- For the Sauce:
- 2 tomatoes, pureed
- 2 tablespoons olive oil
- 1 shallot, chopped
- Sea salt and freshly ground black pepper
- 1/2 teaspoon paprika
- 1/3 cup port wine
- 2 garlic cloves, pressed
- 1/2 lemon, cut into wedges

DIRECTIONS:

1. Grill the clams until they are open, for 5 to 6 minutes.
2. In a frying pan, heat the olive oil over moderate heat. Cook the shallot and garlic until tender and fragrant.
3. Stir in the pureed tomatoes, salt, black pepper, and paprika and continue to cook an additional 10 minutes or until all of them are thoroughly cooked.

4. Heat off and add in the port wine; stir to combine. Garnish with fresh lemon wedges.

NUTRITION: Calories: 134 Fat: 7.8g Carbs: 5.9g Protein: 8.3g

38. Amberjack Fillets with Cheese Sauce

Preparation Time: 0 minutes

Cooking Time: 20 minutes

Servings: 6

INGREDIENTS:

- 6 amberjack fillets
- 1/4 cup fresh tarragon chopped
- 2 tablespoons olive oil, at room temperature
- Sea salt and ground black pepper
- For the Sauce:
- 1/3 cup vegetable broth
- 3/4 cup double cream
- 1/3 cup Romano cheese, grated
- 3 teaspoons butter, at room temperature
- 2 garlic cloves, finely minced

DIRECTIONS:

1. In a non-stick frying pan, ley the olive oil heat until sizzling.
2. Once hot, fry the amberjack for about 6 minutes per side or until the edges are turning opaque. Sprinkle them with salt, black pepper, and tarragon. Reserve.
3. To make the sauce, melt the butter in a saucepan over moderately high heat. Sauté the garlic until tender and fragrant or about 2 minutes.
4. Add in the vegetable broth and cream and continue to cook for 5 to 6 minutes more; heat off.
5. Stir in the Romano cheese and continue stirring in the residual heat for a couple of minutes more.

NUTRITION: Calories: 285 Fat: 20.4g Carbs: 1.2g Protein: 23.8g

39. Refreshing Prawn Salad

Preparation Time: 5 minutes

Cooking Time: 5 minutes

Servings: 6

INGREDIENTS:

- 2 pounds tiger prawns, peeled leaving tails intact
- Sea salt and freshly ground black pepper
- 1 celery rib, sliced
- 1 cup white onions, chopped
- 1 Lebanese cucumber, chopped
- 1/2 head Iceberg lettuce, torn into pieces
- 1/4 cup fresh basil, chopped
- Juice from 1 fresh lime
- 1/4 cup capers, drained
- 1/2 cup mayonnaise

DIRECTIONS:

1. Boil the tiger prawns in a large pot of salted water for about 3 minutes. Drain well and let it cool completely.
2. Pour the remaining ingredients into a huge bowl; toss to combine well.

NUTRITION: Calories: 196 Fat: 8.3g Carbs: 6.5g Protein: 21.4g

40. Middle-Eastern Salmon with Nabulsi Cheese

Preparation Time: 5 minutes

Cooking Time: 15 minutes

Servings: 6

INGREDIENTS:

- 6 salmon fillets
- 1 garlic clove, finely minced
- 1 cup Nabulsi cheese, crumbled
- 3 tablespoons mayonnaise
- Coarse salt and black pepper, to taste
- 1 teaspoon Za'atar
- 1 cup cauliflower
- 1/2 cup shallots, thinly sliced
- 1 tablespoon fresh lemon juice
- 2 tablespoons sesame oil

DIRECTIONS:

1. Toss the salmon fillets with salt, pepper, and Za'atar. Place the salmon fillets on a parchment-lined baking pan; scatter the cauliflower, shallot, and garlic around the fish fillets.
2. Wrap with the foil and bake in the preheated oven at 390 degrees F for 10 to 12 minutes or until the salmon fillets flake easily with a fork. Remove the foil.
3. Mix the Nabulsi cheese, mayonnaise, lemon juice, and sesame oil. Put the cheese mixture over the fish and vegetables.
4. Bake for a further 5 minutes or until the top is hot and bubbly.

NUTRITION: Calories: 354 Fat: 20.2g Carbs: 4.5g Protein: 39.6g

41. Red Snapper Soup

Preparation Time: 5 minutes

Cooking Time: 20 minutes

Servings: 4

INGREDIENTS:

- 1 pound red snapper, chopped
- 1 cup tomato puree
- 3 cups chicken stock
- 1/4 cup Marsala wine
- 2 thyme sprigs, chopped
- 1/2 teaspoon dried rosemary
- 1/2 stick butter, melted
- 1 medium leek, finely chopped
- 2 garlic cloves, minced
- 1/4 cup fresh parsley, chopped
- Sea salt and ground black pepper

DIRECTIONS:

1. In a heavy-bottomed pot, let the butter melt over moderately high heat—Cook the leek and garlic for 4 minutes or until they become tender and fragrant.
2. Add in the parsley, tomato puree, chicken stock, wine, red snapper, and rosemary; bring to a rolling boil.
3. Turn the heat to simmer; continue until they are thoroughly cooked for a further 15 to 20 minutes—season with salt and pepper to taste.

NUTRITION: Calories: 316 Fat: 14.3g Carbs: 6.6g Protein: 32.7g

42. **Family Seafood Bowl**

Preparation Time: 7 minutes

Cooking Time: 3 minutes

Servings: 4

INGREDIENTS:

- 1 pound sea scallops, halved horizontally
- 1/2 cup Kalamata olives, sliced
- 2 cups arugula
- 1/2 tablespoon Dijon mustard
- 1 teaspoon garlic, chopped
- 1 cup cherry tomatoes, halved
- 1 Lebanese cucumber, sliced
- 1/4 cup extra-virgin olive oil
- 2 tablespoons fresh lime juice
- Sea salt and pepper, to season

DIRECTIONS:

1. Boil the scallops in a pot of lightly salted water for about 3 minutes or until opaque; place them in a serving bowl.
2. To make the salad, toss the remaining ingredients until everything is well combined.

NUTRITION: Calories: 260 Fat: 13.6g Carbs: 5.9g Protein: 28.1g

43. **Tilapia with Spicy Dijon Sauce**

Preparation Time: 2 hours

Cooking Time: 5 minutes

Servings: 4

INGREDIENTS:

- 1 tablespoon butter, room temperature
- 2 chili peppers, deveined and minced
- 1 cup heavy cream
- 1 teaspoon Dijon mustard
- 1 pound tilapia fish, cubed
- Sea salt and ground black pepper
- 1 cup white onions, chopped
- 1 teaspoon garlic, pressed
- 1/2 cup dark rum

DIRECTIONS:

1. Toss the tilapia with salt, pepper, onions, garlic, chili peppers, and rum. Let it marinate for 2 hours in your refrigerator.
2. In a grill pan, melt the butter over moderately high heat. Sear the fish in hot butter, basting with the reserved marinade.
3. Add in the mustard and cream and continue to cook until everything is thoroughly cooked for 2 to 3 minutes.

NUTRITION: Calories: 228 Fat: 13g Carbs: 6.5g Protein: 13.7g

44. **Rich and Spicy Seafood Stew**

Preparation Time: 5 minutes

Cooking Time: 25 minutes

Servings: 4

INGREDIENTS:

- 1/2 pound sole, cut into 2-inch pieces
- 1/3 pound halibut, cut into 2-inch pieces
- 1/2 cup Marsala wine
- 1/8 teaspoon hot sauce

- 1 tablespoon lard, room temperature
- 1 cup shallots, chopped
- 1 teaspoon garlic, smashed
- Sea salt and black pepper, to taste
- 4 cups of chicken bone broth
- 1 cup tomato sauce
- 2 thyme sprigs, chopped

DIRECTIONS:

1. In a large-sized pot, melt the lard over medium-high heat. Cook the garlic and shallots until they turn soft.
2. Add in the salt, black pepper, chicken bone broth, tomato sauce, and thyme and; continue to cook an additional 15 minutes.
3. Add in the fish, wine, and hot sauce; bring to a boil. Reduce the heat to simmer for 4 to 5 minutes longer, stirring periodically.

NUTRITION: Calories: 296 Fat: 8.6g Carbs: 5.5g Protein: 41.4g

POULTRY

45. Bacon-Wrapped Chicken with Grilled Asparagus

Preparation Time: 20 minutes

Cooking Time: 25 minutes

Servings: 4

INGREDIENTS:

- 6 chicken breasts
- Pink salt and black pepper to taste
- 8 bacon slices
- 3 tbsp olive oil
- 1 lb asparagus spears
- 3 tbsp olive oil
- 2 tbsp fresh lemon juice
- Manchego cheese for topping

DIRECTIONS:

1. Preheat the oven to 400°F.
2. Flavor chicken breasts with black pepper and salt, and wrap 2 bacon slices around each chicken breast.
3. Arrange on a baking sheet that is lined with parchment paper, drizzle with oil and bake for 25 to 30 minutes until the bacon turns brown and crispy.
4. Preheat your grill to high heat.
5. Put the olive oil all over the the asparagus spears and season with salt.
6. Grill for 8-10 minutes, frequently turning until slightly charred.
7. Move to a clean plate and drizzle with lemon juice. Grate over Manchego cheese so that it melts a little on contact with the hot asparagus and forms a cheesy dressing.

NUTRITION: Calories: 468 cal Fat: 38g Carbs: 2g Protein: 26g Fiber:

46. Spinach Chicken Cheesy Bake

Preparation Time: 20 minutes

Cooking Time: 25 minutes

Servings: 6

INGREDIENTS:

- 6 chicken breasts, skinless and boneless
- 1 tsp mixed spice seasoning
- Pink salt and black pepper to season
- 2 loose cups baby spinach
- 3 tsp olive oil
- 4 oz cream cheese, cubed
- 1 ¼ cups shredded mozzarella cheese
- 4 tbsp water

DIRECTIONS:

1. Preheat oven to 370°F.
2. Season chicken with spice mix, salt, and black pepper.
3. Pat with your hands to have the seasoning stick on the chicken.
4. Put in the casserole dish and layer spinach over the chicken.
5. Mix the oil with cream cheese, mozzarella, salt, and black pepper and stir in water a tablespoon at a time.
6. Put the mixture above the chicken and cover the pot with an aluminum foil.
7. Bake for 20 minutes, get rid of the foil and continue cooking for 15 minutes until a nice golden brown color is formed on top.
8. Take out and allow sitting for 5 minutes. Serve warm with braised asparagus.

NUTRITION: Calories: 340 cal Fat: 30.2g Carbs: 3.1g Protein: 15g Fiber:

47. Parmesan Wings with Yogurt Sauce

Preparation Time: 5 minutes

Cooking Time: 20 minutes

Servings: 6

INGREDIENTS:

- For the Dipping Sauce
- 1 cup plain yogurt
- 1 tsp fresh lemon juice
- Salt and black pepper to taste
- For the Wings
- 2 lb chicken wings
- Salt and black pepper to taste
- Cooking spray
- ½ cup melted butter
- ½ cup Hot sauce
- ¼ cup grated Parmesan cheese

DIRECTIONS:

1. Mix the yogurt, lemon juice, salt, and black pepper in a bowl. Chill while making the chicken.
2. Preheat oven to 400°F and season wings with salt and black pepper.
3. Line them on a baking sheet and grease lightly with cooking spray.
4. Bake for 20 minutes until golden brown.
5. Mix butter, hot sauce, and Parmesan cheese in a bowl.
6. Toss chicken in the sauce to evenly coat and plate.
7. Serve with yogurt dipping sauce and celery strips.

NUTRITION: Calories: 452 Fat: 36.4g Carbs: 4g Protein: 24g Fiber:

48. Eggplant & Tomato Braised Chicken Thighs

Preparation Time: 25 minutes

Cooking Time: 20 minutes

Servings: 4

INGREDIENTS:

- 2 tbsp ghee
- 1 lb chicken thighs
- Salt and black pepper to taste
- 2 cloves garlic, minced
- 1 (14 oz) can whole tomatoes
- 1 eggplant, diced
- 10 fresh basil leaves, chopped + extra to garnish

DIRECTIONS:

1. Melt ghee in a saucepan over medium heat, season the chicken with salt and black pepper and fry for 4 minutes on each side until golden brown. Remove to a plate.
2. Sauté the garlic in the ghee for 2 minutes, pour in the tomatoes, and cook covered for 8 minutes.
3. Add in the eggplant and basil—Cook for 4 minutes. Season the sauce with salt and black pepper, stir and add the chicken. Coat with sauce and simmer for 3 minutes.
4. Serve chicken with sauce on a bed of squash pasta. Garnish with extra basil

NUTRITION: Calories: 468 Fat: 39.5g Carbs: 2g Protein: 26g Fiber:

49. Lemon Threaded Chicken Skewers

Preparation Time: 2 hours

Cooking Time: 10 minutes

Servings: 4

INGREDIENTS:

- 3 chicken breasts, cut into cubes
- 2 tbsp olive oil, divided
- 2/3 jar preserved lemon, flesh removed, drained
- 2 cloves garlic, minced
- ½ cup lemon juice
- Salt and black pepper to taste
- 1 tsp rosemary leaves to garnish
- 2 to 4 lemon wedges to garnish

DIRECTIONS:

1. First, thread the chicken onto skewers and set aside.
2. In a wide bowl, mix half of the oil, garlic, salt, pepper, and lemon juice, and add the chicken skewers, and lemon rind.
3. Put a cover on the bowl and allow the chicken to marinate for at least 2 hours in the refrigerator.
4. When the marinating time is almost over, preheat a grill to 350°F, and remove the chicken onto the grill. Cook for 6 minutes on each side.
5. Remove and serve warm garnished with rosemary leaves and lemons wedges.

NUTRITION: Calories: 350 Fat: 11g Carbs: 3.5g Protein: 34g Fiber:

50. **Creamy Stuffed Chicken with Parma Ham**

Preparation Time: 10 minutes

Cooking Time: 30 minutes

Servings: 4

INGREDIENTS:

- 4 chicken breasts
- 2 tbsp olive oil
- 3 cloves garlic, minced
- 3 shallots, finely chopped
- 4 tbsp dried mixed herbs
- 8 slices Parma ham
- 8 oz cream cheese
- 2 lemons, zested
- Salt to taste

DIRECTIONS:

1. Preheat the oven to 350°F.
2. Put and heat the oil in a skillet and fry the garlic and shallots with a pinch of salt and lemon zest for 3 minutes; let it cool. After, stir the cream cheese and mixed herbs into the shallot mixture.

3. Score a pocket in each chicken breast, fill the holes with the cream cheese mixture and cover with the cut-out chicken.
4. Wrap each breast with two Parma ham and secure the ends with a toothpick.
5. Lay the chicken parcels on a greased baking sheet and cook in the oven for 20 minutes.
6. Remove to rest for 4 minutes before serving with a green salad and roasted tomatoes.

NUTRITION: Calories: 485 Fat: 35g Carbs: 2g, Protein: 26g

51. **Chicken Drumsticks in Tomato Sauce**

Preparation Time: 30 minutes

Cooking Time: 1 hour

Servings: 4

INGREDIENTS:

- 8 chicken drumsticks
- 1 ½ tbsp olive oil
- 1 medium white onion, diced
- 3 medium turnips, peeled and diced
- 2 medium carrots, chopped in 1-inch pieces
- 2 green bell peppers, seeded, sliced into chunks
- 2 cloves garlic, minced
- ¼ cup coconut flour
- 1 cup chicken broth
- 1 (28 oz) can sugar-free tomato sauce
- 2 tbsp dried Italian herbs
- Salt and black pepper to taste

DIRECTIONS:

1. Preheat oven to 400°F.
2. Put some oil in a skillet and allow it to heat over medium fire, meanwhile season the drumsticks with pepper and salt then fry in

the oil to brown on both sides for 10 minutes.

3. Remove to a baking dish. Sauté the onion, turnips, bell peppers, carrots, and garlic in the same oil and for 10 minutes with continuous stirring.

4. In a bowl, combine the broth, coconut flour, tomato paste, and Italian herbs together, and pour it over the vegetables in the pan.

5. Stir and cook to thicken for 4 minutes.

6. Pour the mixture on the chicken in the baking dish—Bake for around 1 hour.

7. Get it off the oven and serve with steamed cauli rice.

NUTRITION: Calories: 515 Fat: 34.2g Carbs: 7.3g Protein: 50.8g Fiber:

52. **Chicken, Broccoli & Cashew Stir-Fry**

Preparation Time: 10 minutes

Cooking Time: 20 minutes

Servings: 4

INGREDIENTS:

- 2 chicken breasts, cut into strips
- 3 tbsp olive oil
- 2 tbsp soy sauce
- 2 tsp white wine vinegar
- 1 tsp erythritol
- 2 tsp xanthan gum
- 1 lemon, juiced
- 1 cup unsalted cashew nuts
- 2 cups broccoli florets
- 1 white onion, thinly sliced
- Salt and black pepper to taste

DIRECTIONS:

1. In a bowl, put the vinegar, soy sauce, lemon juice, erythritol, and xanthan gum together then mix. Set aside.

2. Let the oil heat in a wok and fry the cashew for 4 minutes until golden brown.

3. Remove to a paper towel-lined plate.

4. Sauté the onion in the same oil for 4 minutes until soft and browned; add to the cashew nuts.

5. Put the chicken and cook for 4 minutes; include the broccoli, salt, and black pepper.

6. Stir-fry and pour the soy sauce mixture in. Stir and cook the sauce for 4 minutes and pour in the cashews and onion.

7. Stir once more, cook for 1 minute, and turn the heat off.

8. Serve the chicken stir-fry with some steamed cauli rice.

NUTRITION: Calories: 286 Fat: 10.1g Carbs: 3.4g Protein: 17.3g Fiber:

53. **Cheese Stuffed Chicken Breasts with Spinach**

Preparation Time: 30 minutes

Cooking Time: 20 minutes

Servings: 4

INGREDIENTS:

- 4 chicken breasts, boneless and skinless
- ½ cup mozzarella cheese
- ⅓ cup Parmesan cheese
- 6 ounces cream cheese
- 2 cups spinach, chopped
- A pinch of nutmeg
- ½ tsp minced garlic
- Breading:
- 2 eggs
- ⅓ cup almond flour
- 2 tbsp olive oil
- ½ tsp parsley
- ⅓ cup Parmesan cheese
- A pinch of onion powder

DIRECTIONS:

1. Pound the chicken until it doubles in size.

2. Mix the cream cheese, spinach, mozzarella, nutmeg, salt, black pepper, and Parmesan cheese in a bowl.

3. Divide the mixture into four and spread out evenly into each chicken breast.

4. Wrap the chicken in a plastic wrap. Refrigerate for 15 minutes.

5. Heat the oil in a pan and preheat the oven to 370°F.

6. Beat the eggs and combine all other breading ingredients in a bowl.

7. Put the chicken in egg then in the breading mixture.

8. Cook in the pan until browned. Place on a baking sheet that's lined and bake for 20 minutes.

NUTRITION: Calories: 491 Fat: 36g Carbs: 3.5g Protein: 38g

54. Chili Turkey Patties with Cucumber Salsa

Preparation Time: 10 minutes

Cooking Time: 20 minutes

Servings: 4

INGREDIENTS:

- 2 spring onions, thinly sliced
- 1 pound ground turkey
- 1 egg
- 2 garlic cloves, minced
- 1 tbsp chopped herbs
- 1 small chili pepper, deseeded and diced
- 2 tbsp ghee
- Cucumber Salsa
- 1 tbsp apple cider vinegar
- 1 tbsp chopped dill
- 1 garlic clove, minced
- 2 cucumbers, grated
- 1 cup sour cream
- 1 jalapeño pepper, minced
- 2 tbsp olive oil

DIRECTIONS:

1. Place all turkey ingredients, except the ghee, in a bowl. Mix to combine.

2. Make patties out of the mixture.

3. Put the ghee in a skillet over medium heat until it melts. Cook the patties for 3 minutes per side.

4. Put all the salsa ingredients inside a bowl and mix to combine. Serve the patties topped with salsa.

NUTRITION: Calories: 475 Fat: 38g Carbs: 5g Protein: 26g Fiber:

MEAT

55. Lemon Butter Pork Chops

Preparation time: 5 minutes

Cooking time: 25 minutes

Servings: 4

INGREDIENTS:

- ½ teaspoon of sea salt
- 1 teaspoon lemon-pepper seasoning
- 1 teaspoon garlic powder
- ½ teaspoon dried thyme
- 4 (4-ounce) boneless pork chops
- 5 tablespoons butter, divided
- ¼ cup Bone Broth
- 2 tablespoons freshly squeezed lemon juice
- 1 tablespoon minced garlic
- ½ cup heavy (whipping) cream

DIRECTIONS:

1. In a small bowl, put and stir the lemon-pepper seasoning, salt, thyme, and garlic powder.
2. Brush the spice mixture all around the pork chops.
3. Get a skillet and heat it over medium-high heat then melt down 2 tablespoons of butter.
4. Put the pork chops then cook for at least 5 minutes on each side until they are cooked through.
5. Remove the chops from the pan.
6. Reduce the heat to medium-low.
7. Put the bone broth, garlic, lemon juice, and the remaining 3 tablespoons of butter.
8. Put the pork chops and seethe for about 15 minutes, add the cream 1 tablespoon every few minutes, or up until the sauce turns thick.
9. Remove from the heat and serve.

NUTRITION: Calories: 379 Fat: 29g Carbs: 2.5g Protein: 27g

56. Fully Loaded Burger Bowls

Preparation time: 15 minutes

Cooking time: 30 minutes

Servings: 4

INGREDIENTS:

- garlic powder (1 tsp)
- extra lean beef (2lb)
- butter (2 tablespoons)
- lawry's seasoned salt (2 ½ tsp)
- ground black pepper (½ tsp)
- sliced mushrooms (2 cups)
- worcestershire sauce (3 tsp)
- shredded cheddar cheese (2 cups)
- cooked bacon (10 slices)
- bbq sauce (for toppings)
- diced chives(for toppings)
- ranch (for toppings)
- diced bacon (for toppings)

DIRECTIONS:

1. Mix up the beef, garlic powder, Worcestershire sauce, seasoned salt, and black pepper in a bowl.
2. Line a baking sheet with a foil and neatly arrange four meat bowls on it. Use a clean can to make the bowls.
3. Get a small pan and shallow fry the mushrooms in butter. Add some pepper and salt for taste. Now divide into 4 parts.
4. Now it's time to fill your meat bowls. Pour in a bit of cheese, diced bacon, mushrooms, and pour the rest of the cheese on top of all these.
5. Leave to bake at 350°F loosely covered for about 30 minutes.
6. Add your toppings: BBQ sauce, diced chives, ranch, and diced bacon.

NUTRITION: Calories: 690 Fats: 49g Carbs: 4g Protein: 71g

57. <u>Roasted Lamb Rack</u>

Preparation time: 20 minutes

Cooking time: 20 minutes

Servings: 4

INGREDIENTS:

- 2 tablespoons fresh rosemary, chopped
- 2 tablespoons garlic, minced
- ¼ cup coconut flour
- 1 tablespoon Dijon mustard
- ¼ teaspoon black pepper
- 4 tablespoons olive oil, divided
- 1 teaspoon salt
- 1 (7 bone) rack of lamb, trimmed
- Salt and freshly ground black pepper

DIRECTIONS:

1. Preheat the oven to 450°F.
2. Add the rosemary, garlic, flour, mustard, ¼ teaspoon black pepper, 2 tablespoons of olive oil, and 1 teaspoon of salt in a large bowl. Mix well until well combined and set aside.
3. On a flat work surface, season the lamb rack with salt and black pepper on both sides.
4. In a skillet over high heat, heat the remaining olive oil until shimmering. Sear the lamb rack for 2 minutes per side. Remove from the heat and brush the rosemary mixture over the lamb rack.
5. Wrap the lamb rack with aluminum foil and place it in a baking sheet.
6. Cook in the heated oven for approximately 15 minutes until the internal temperature reads 145°F (63°C) on a meat thermometer.
7. Take away from the oven and cool for 5 to 7 minutes before serving.

NUTRITION: Calories: 736 Fat: 56.2g Carbs: 6.0g Protein: 51.5g

58. <u>Braised Beef Brisket</u>

Preparation time: 15 minutes

Cooking time: 5 hours and 10 minutes

Servings: 10

INGREDIENTS:

- 1 (5-pound / 2.3-kg) flat-cut corned beef brisket
- 2 tablespoons coconut aminos, or more as needed
- 2 tablespoons olive oil, or more as needed
- 6 garlic cloves, sliced
- 1 onion, sliced
- 2 tablespoons water

DIRECTIONS:

1. Preheat the oven to 275°F.
2. In a bowl, coat the beef brisket with coconut aminos generously.
3. In a huge skillet over medium-high temperature, heat the olive oil until it shimmers.
4. Sear this beef brisket for 5 minutes per side. Transfer to a roasting pan and then add the garlic, onion, and water.
5. Tightly cover the pan with aluminum foil. Put inside the preheated oven and roast for about 5 hours until tender.
6. Let cool for about 10 minutes before slicing to serve.

NUTRITION: Calories: 645 Fat: 51.73g Carbs: 1.3g Protein: 40.4g

59. <u>Beef Chuck Roast</u>

Preparation time: 5 minutes

Cooking time: 8 hours

Servings: 4

INGREDIENTS

- 1 (1-ounce / 28-g) package dry onion soup mix
- ⅓ cup coconut aminos
- 3 pounds (1.4 kg) beef chuck roast
- 2 teaspoons freshly ground black pepper

DIRECTIONS:

1. Add the dry onion soup mix and coconut aminos to a slow cooker, then mix well. Add the beef chuck roast and pour in the water until ½ inch of the roast is covered.
2. Sprinkle with ground black pepper, then cover the lid. Cook on low heat for about 8 hours or until the meat is fork-tender.
3. Confiscate from the heat and cut into slices to serve.

NUTRITION: Calories: 436 Fat: 19.2g Carbs: 3.7g Protein: 60.9g

60. Saucy Pernil Pork

Preparation time: 20 minutes

Cooking time: 6 hours

Servings: 6

INGREDIENTS:

- 4 garlic cloves
- 2 tablespoons fresh oregano, chopped
- 1 large onion, quartered
- 2 teaspoons salt
- 1 tablespoon ground cumin
- 2 teaspoons ground ancho chile pepper
- 2 teaspoons ground black pepper
- 1 tablespoon white wine vinegar
- 1 tablespoon olive oil, or as needed
- 1 (3-pound / 1.4-kg) boneless pork loin roast
- 1 lime, cut into wedges

DIRECTIONS:

1. Add the garlic, oregano, onion, salt, cumin, chile pepper, black pepper, vinegar, and

olive to a food processor, then blend until all the ingredients are fully combined.
2. Rub the mixture around the pork loin, and transfer to a slow cooker.
3. Cover then cook on low heat for about 6 to 8 hours until cooked through.
4. When ready to serve, slice the pork loin to small chunks. Garnish with lime wedges on top before serving.

NUTRITION: Calories: 485 Fat: 22.6g Carbs: 6.7g Protein: 61.1g

61. Creamy Pork Tenderloin

Preparation time: 15 minutes

Cooking time: 35 minutes

Servings: 4

INGREDIENTS:

- 2 tablespoons olive oil
- 2 tablespoons fresh sage, chopped
- 2 tablespoons sun-dried tomatoes, chopped
- 2 tablespoons fresh parsley, chopped
- ¼ cup onion, chopped
- ¼ cup prosciutto, chopped
- 1½ pounds (680 g) pork tenderloin, cut into ½-inch strips
- ½ cup heavy cream
- ½ cup chicken broth
- ¼ teaspoon salt

DIRECTIONS:

1. Take a suitable skillet and place it over medium-high heat. Add the oil to heat then add the sage, tomatoes, parsley, onion, and prosciutto.
2. Sauté the veggies for 5 minutes until soft, then add the pork tenderloin strips to sear for 5 minutes per side.
3. Pour in the heavy cream and broth, then add the salt. Boil the gravy, then reduce the heat to low. Cook for 20 minutes, while

stirring from time to time, or until the sauce thickens. Serve warm.

NUTRITION: Calories: 330 Fat: 18.2g Carbs: 2.8g Protein: 39.5g

62. __Italian Sausage Satay__

Preparation time: 15 minutes

Cooking time: 25 minutes

Servings: 6

INGREDIENTS:

- 6 (4-ounce / 113-g) links Italian sausage
- 2 tablespoons butter
- 4 garlic cloves, minced
- ½ red onion, sliced
- 1 yellow onion, sliced
- 1 green bell pepper, sliced
- 1 large red bell pepper, sliced
- 1 teaspoon dried oregano
- 1 teaspoon dried basil
- ¼ cup white wine

DIRECTIONS:

1. Place a large skillet over medium heat.
2. Put the sausage on the hot skillet and cook until it is browned.
3. Transfer the sausage to a plate and cut into slices.
4. Add the butter in the skillet and heat to melt.
5. Toss in the garlic, red onion, and yellow onion.
6. Sauté for about 3 minutes, then add the green bell pepper, red bell pepper, oregano, basil, and white wine. Cook them until the onions are soft.
7. Put the sausage back to the skillet and reduce the heat to low, then continue cooking covered for about 15 minutes until warmed through.
8. Remove from the heat and serve hot.

NUTRITION: Calories: 461 Fat: 39.4g Carbs: 9.0g Protein: 17.1g

63. __Seasoned Pork Chops__

Preparation time: 10 minutes

Cooking time: 15 minutes

Servings: 8

INGREDIENTS:

- 2 garlic cloves, minced
- Freshly ground black pepper, to taste
- 1 lime, juiced
- 1 tablespoon fresh basil, chopped
- 1 tablespoon Old Bay seafood seasoning
- ½ cup apple cider vinegar
- ½ cup olive oil
- 8 boneless pork chops, cut into ½ inch thick

DIRECTIONS:

1. Add the minced garlic, black pepper, lime juice, basil, seasoning, apple cider vinegar, and olive oil to a Ziploc bag.
2. Place the pork chops in this bag and seal it.
3. Shake it well to coat the pork and place it in the refrigerator for 6 hours.
4. Continue flipping and shaking the bag every 1 hour.
5. Meanwhile, preheat your outdoor grill over medium-high heat.
6. Remove the pork chops from the Ziploc bag and discard its marinade.
7. Grill all the marinated pork chops for 7 minutes per side until their internal temperature reaches 145°F (63°C). Serve warm on a plate.

NUTRITION: Calories: 412 Fat: 26.4g Carbs: 1.0g Protein: 40.0g

64. __Garlicky Pork Roast__

Preparation time: 20 minutes

Cooking time: 2 hours

Servings: 6

INGREDIENTS:

- 3 pounds (1.4 kg) pork tenderloin
- 2 garlic cloves, minced
- 1 tablespoon olive oil
- 3 tablespoons dried rosemary

DIRECTIONS:

1. Preheat the oven to 375°F.
2. Mix the olive oil, garlic, and rosemary in a bowl, then rub this mixture all over the pork tenderloin.
3. Put the pork tenderloin in a roasting pan and roast in the preheated oven for about 2 hours or up until the inside temperature reaches 145°F (63°C).
4. Once roasted, remove the tenderloin from the oven. Slice and serve warm.

NUTRITION: Calories: 274 Fat: 7.4g Carbs: 1.4g Protein: 47.7g

65. Spiced Pork Tenderloin

Preparation time: 10 minutes

Cooking time: 2 hours

Servings: 4

INGREDIENTS:

- 2 teaspoons minced garlic
- 1 tablespoon fresh cilantro
- 1 dash ground black pepper
- 2½ teaspoons ground cumin
- 1 teaspoon salt
- 2 tablespoons chili powder
- 2 pounds (907g) pork tenderloin, cubed

DIRECTIONS:

1. In a bowl, add the garlic, cilantro, black pepper, cumin, salt, and chili powder. Mix these spices together.
2. Toss in the pork cubes and coat them well with the spice mixture.

3. Cover the pork cubes and refrigerate them for 45 minutes to marinate.
4. Meanwhile, preheat the oven to 225°F (107°C).
5. Arrange the spiced pork in a baking tray and roast for 2 hours, or until crispy.
6. Remove from the oven and serve on a plate.

NUTRITION: Calories: 291 Fat: 8.9g Carbs: 3.1g Protein: 47.7g

66. Basil-Rubbed Pork Chops

Preparation time: 15 minutes

Cooking time: 25 minutes

Servings: 4

INGREDIENTS:

- 4 (8-ounce / 227-g) pork chops
- 1 lime, juiced
- ¼ cup fresh basil, chopped
- 4 garlic cloves, minced
- Salt and freshly ground black pepper
- 1 tablespoon olive oil

DIRECTIONS:

1. Put the pork chops in a baking tray and drizzle lime juice over them to coat. Rub the basil, garlic, salt, and black pepper over the chops.
2. Cover the chops and let stand for about 30 minutes.
3. For the meantime, preheat an outdoor grill on medium heat and lightly grease its grate with olive oil.
4. Transfer the marinated pork chops to the grill and cook for 10 minutes per side until the inside temperature reaches 145°F (63°C).
5. Let cool for about 5 minutes before serving.

NUTRITION: Calories: 512 Fat: 28.5g Carbs: 2.1g Protein: 58.4g

VEGETABLES

67. Grilled Sandwich Cheese

Preparation Time: 5 minutes

Cooking Time: 15 minutes

Servings: 1

INGREDIENTS:

- 2 Grand Eggs
- 2 Spoonfuls of almond flour
- 1 1/2 cubic pound psyllium husk powder
- 1/2 cup of baking powder
- 2 Soft butter spoons
- 2 Units of Cheddar Cheese
- 1 Pound of butter

DIRECTIONS:

1. Combine all of the bun ingredients in one jar. Continue mixing until heavy.
2. Slowly pour into a square jar or cup, and flatten it. Clean the sides if need be.
3. Microwave for 90 seconds, and test if this is done. If not, carry on in intervals of 15 seconds.
4. Take the break out of the container after cooking, and cut in half.
5. Place the cheese between the buns, heat the butter in a saucepan over medium heat, and fry the grilled cheese until the texture satisfies.

NUTRITION: Calories: 803 Fat: 70g Carbs: 6.14g Protein: 25.84g

68. New Basil Pizza With Paprika

Preparation Time: 10 minutes

Cooking Time: 25 minutes

Servings: 2

INGREDIENTS:

- 6 Mozzarella cheese
- 1/2 cup almond meal
- 2 Tablespoons of a husk of psyllium
- 2 Spoonfuls of cream cheese
- 2 Cooked lbs of fresh parmesan
- 1 Egg
- 1/2 cup of salt
- 1/2 Teaspoon chili pepper

DIRECTIONS:

1. Preheat the oven to 400°F.
2. Microwave mozzarella cheese until melted and pliable to the maximum.
3. Apply the majority of the pizza ingredients (with the exception of the topping) to the cheese and blend well.
4. To flatten the dough, use your hands or a rolling pin and form a circle.
5. Bake the pizza for 10 minutes and remove it from the oven.
6. Place the toppings over the pizza and bake for another 8-10 minutes.
7. Allow the pizza to cool down before serving.

NUTRITION: Calories: 411 Fat: 31g Carbs: 6g Protein: 22g

69. Splendid Jalapeno Poppers

Preparation Time: 10 minutes

Cooking Time: 25 minutes

Servings: 8

INGREDIENTS:

- 5 Units Cream Cheese
- 1/4 Tasse of mozzarella
- 8 Medium peppered jalapeno
- 1/4 liter of salt
- 1/4 Teaspoon chili pepper
- Ms. Dash table mix with 1/2 teaspoon

- 8 Bacon slices

DIRECTIONS:

1. Oven preheats to 400F. Cut all of the jalapenos in half, and use a knife to remove the peppers' "guts."
2. Mix the cream cheese, mozzarella, and your seasoning range in a mug.
3. Pack the mixture of cream cheese in peppers, and place the other half of the pepper on top to close the peppers.
4. In 1 slice of bacon, wrap each pepper, starting from the bottom and working up.
5. Bake 20-25 minutes and then fry for 2-3 minutes.

NUTRITION: Calories: 121 Fat: 10g Carbs: 2g Protein: 5g

70. **Personal Pizzas In Portobello**

Preparation Time: 15 minutes

Cooking Time: 10 minutes

Servings: 4

INGREDIENTS:

- 4 Big caps of champignon portobello
- 1 Good Tomato wine
- 4 Ounces of fresh cheese mozzarella
- 1/4 cup freshly cut basil
- 6 The olive oil spoon
- 20 Slices of moist chilies
- Great for salt and pepper

DIRECTIONS:

1. Scrape out the mushroom innards and keep scraping the meat out until the mushroom shell is all you have left.
2. Take the oven to the grill and clean with about 3 tablespoons the tops of all the mushrooms: olive oil, Olive oil. Sprinkle with oil and season with salt and pepper.
3. Fry the mushrooms, turn them over and repeat the process for about 4-5 minutes.

4. Cut the tomatoes into thin slices-12-16 slices is enough. Place the tomato on top of the mushrooms, and add the basil.
5. Apply pepperoni to each slice, and sliced mozzarella. Fry for an extra 2-4 minutes, or until the cheese melts and begins browning.
6. Remove and allow to cool.

NUTRITION: Calories: 339 Fat: 32g Carbs: 4g Protein: 10g

71. **Green Vegetarian Coconut Curry**

Preparation Time: 5 minutes

Cooking Time: 15 minutes

Servings: 2

INGREDIENTS:

- 1 Cup of broccoli blossoms
- 1 Great Pack of Spinach
- 4 Cups of coconut oil
- 1/4 Mean Onion
- 1 Teaspoon of chopped garlic
- 1 Teaspoon Cut Ginger
- 2 Cups of Fysh sauce
- 2 Cups of soy sauce
- 1 Twin cubit red curry paste
- 1/2 cup cream for coconut (or milk for coconut)

DIRECTIONS:

1. Split the chopped garlic and the onions. Add 2 dc. Pour coconut oil into a saucepan and heat to medium-high.
2. Attach the onions to the pan after heating, and cook semi-transparently. Then add the garlic to brown in the pan.
3. Switch to medium-low heat and add broccoli to plate. Stir it all up nicely.
4. When the broccoli is cooked in part, transfer the vegetables to the side of the

saucepan and add the curry paste. Let it cook within 45-60 seconds.

5. Add spinach to the broccoli and add the coconut cream and the remaining coconut oil once it begins to willow.

6. Add soy sauce, fish sauce, and ginger and mix well. Simmer according to the desired thickness for 5-10 minutes.

NUTRITION: Calories: 398 Fat: 41g Carbs: 8g Protein: 4g

72. <u>Pork Shiitake With "Fast Kimchi" Stir Fry</u>

Preparation Time: 15 minutes

Cooking Time: 30 minutes

Servings: 4

INGREDIENTS:

- Hope Kimchi
- 3 Cups of purple chopped cabbage
- 3 Cups of rice vinegar
- 1 cup of minced garlic
- 2 Chopped Ginger Teaspoons
- 1 1/2 cubic lb Red Boat Fish Sauce
- 2 Teaspoons with red potato flakes
- 1/3 Full Radish daikon
- 1 Giant Shallot
- 1 Medium red pepper
- 1 Twin cubit red curry paste
- 1 1/2 teaspoon soy sauce (or amino acids from the coconut)
- Stir the ingredients into the fry
- 1 pound fresh pork
- 3 Lbs of coconut oil
- 3 1/2 ounces of champignons shiitake
- 1 Giant Shallot
- 2 Cups of white wine
- 1 tablespoon of erythritol NOW
- 1 1 1/2 cubit sesame oil
- Great for salt and pepper

DIRECTIONS:

1. Split the chili and cabbage into thin strips. Split the radish of daikon into matches.

2. Combine all the ingredients of "Fast Kimchi" in a pot, and blend well. Set aside while the pork is being prepared.

3. Cut the pork loin into thin medallions (approx. 1/4 "thick). Apply 1 tablespoon of coconut oil on both sides to cook half the pork before the brown spots emerge.

4. Cut the pork and put it on aside. Then make 1 tbsp to the second batch. Less olive oil.

5. Placed "kimchi" in the saucepan and let the juices boil for 4-5 minutes. Again add pork (with oil) and stir well, allow to cook for another few minutes.

NUTRITION: Calories: 322 Fat: 18g Carbs: 8g Protein: 28g

73. <u>Avocado Stuffed With Egg Salad</u>

Preparation Time: 20 minutes

Cooking Time: 0 minutes

Servings: 3

INGREDIENTS:

- 6 Hard-boiled, big eggs
- 1/3 Half red onion
- 3 Celery Ribs
- 4 Cups of mayonnaise
- 2 Black Mustard Teaspoons
- 2 Spoonfuls of pure lime juice
- 1 Löffel hot sauce
- 1/2 Cumin Teaspoon
- Great for salt and pepper
- 3 Large Lawyers

DIRECTIONS:

1. Prepare all ingredients by cutting the eggs, onions, and celery into bits.

2. Add all the ingredients, excluding avocado, in a dish.
3. Cut the avocado off, and through the seed.
4. Place the avocado egg salad in.

NUTRITION: Calories: 281 Fat: 25g Carbs: 3g Protein: 8g

74. **Cheesy Waffles With Thyme**

Preparation Time: 20 minutes

Cooking Time: 10 minutes

Servings: 4

INGREDIENTS:

- ½ big, mature cauliflower
- 1 Cup of fine-cut mozzarella
- 1 Cup Packed with Collard Greens
- 1/3 tablespoon Parmesan cheese
- 2 Grand Eggs
- 2 Spring-onion sticks
- 1 Twin cubit sesame seed
- 1 spoonful of olive oil
- 2 Freshly chopped spoonful of thyme
- 1 Teaspoon Ail Dust
- ½ teaspoon hot chili pepper
- ½ cup of salt

DIRECTIONS:

1. Rice the cauliflower by pulsing the florets in a food processor until it reaches a crumbly texture.
2. Add the chopped vegetables, spring onions, and thyme and pulse a few more times until all is mixed well.

3. Pour the mixture into a mixing bowl, add the remaining ingredients, and combine well.
4. When dry, pour in the mixture uniformly over a waffle iron frying pan.
5. Cook the mixture until it forms a waffle then remove it.

NUTRITION: Calories: 203 Fat: 15g Carbs: 6g Protein: 15g

75. **Simple Omelet Recette**

Preparation Time: 5 minutes

Cooking Time: 10 minutes

Servings: 4

INGREDIENTS:

- Butter 50 g
- 7 Eggs on pcs
- 3 Tbsp dairy
- 7 Pinch salt

DIRECTIONS:

1. Whisk the beans, salt, and milk together with a fork in a mixing dish. Melt the butter into a saucepan.
2. Put the egg mixture in the saucepan and set it to a low heat a little. Turn the omelet with a spatula, until the surface is just slightly moist.
3. For another 2 minutes, fry the omelet and serve while it's dry.

NUTRITION: Calories: 302 Fat: 10g Carbs: 23g Protein: 27g

SOUPS AND STEWS

76. Chicken Cabbage Soup

Preparation time: 5 minutes

Cooking time: 30 minutes

Servings: 6

INGREDIENTS:

- 1 can Italian-style tomatoes
- 3 cups chicken broth
- 1 chicken breast
- ½ head of cabbage, shredded
- 1 packet Italian seasoning mix

DIRECTIONS:

1. Place a heavy-bottomed pot on medium fire and heat for a minute. Add oil and swirl to coat the bottom and sides of the pot.
2. Pan fry chicken breast for 4 minutes per side. Transfer to a chopping board and cut into ½-inch cubes.
3. Combine all ingredients into the pot and stir well.
4. Boil all the ingredients, lower fire to a simmer, and cook for 20 more minutes.
5. Adjust seasoning to taste, serve, and enjoy.

NUTRITION: Calories: 248 Fat: 9.3g Carbs: 5.6g Protein: 34.1g

77. Corn and Bacon Chowder

Preparation Time: 20 minutes

Cooking Time: 23 minutes

Servings: 8

INGREDIENTS:

- ½ cup bacon, fried and crumbled
- 1 package celery, onion, and bell pepper mix
- 2 cups full-fat milk
- ½ cup sharp cheddar cheese, grated

DIRECTIONS:

1. In a heavy-bottomed pot, melt butter.
2. Saute the bacon and celery for 3 minutes.
3. Turn fire on to medium. Add remaining ingredients and cook for 20 minutes until thick.
4. Serve and enjoy with a sprinkle of crumbled bacon.

NUTRITION Calories: 210.5 Fat: 13.6g Carbs: 4.4g Protein: 16.6g

78. Creamy Cauliflower Soup

Preparation time: 5 minutes

Cooking time: 20 minutes

Servings: 4

INGREDIENTS:

- 1 cauliflower head, chopped
- ½ cup onions, chopped
- 4 cups chicken broth
- 1 tablespoon butter
- 1 cup heavy cream

DIRECTIONS:

1. Combine all of the ingredients in a clean pot and heat over medium-high fire, except for the heavy cream.
2. Season with salt and pepper to taste.
3. Give a good stir to combine everything.
4. Cover and bring to a boil, and simmer for 15 minutes.
5. With an immersion blender, blend well until smooth and creamy.
6. Stir in heavy cream then simmer for another 5 minutes. Adjust seasoning if needed.
7. Serve and enjoy.

NUTRITION Calories: 531 Fat: 30.8g Carbs: 7.3g Protein: 53.9g

79. Tomato Hamburger Soup

Preparation time: 10 minutes

Cooking time: 25 minutes

Servings: 8

INGREDIENTS:

- 1-pound ground beef
- 1 can V-8 juice
- 2 packages frozen vegetable mix
- 1 can condensed mushroom soup
- 2 teaspoon dried onion powder

DIRECTIONS:

1. Place a pot over medium heat for 2 minutes. Add oil and heat for a minute.
2. Sauté the beef until lightly browned, around 7 minutes—season with salt, pepper, and onion powder.
3. Add the mushroom soup and water.
4. Give a good stir to combine everything.
5. Cover the pot and continue to heat until it boils inside.
6. Lower fire to a simmer and cook for 10 minutes.
7. Stir in vegetables. Cook until heated through around 5 minutes. Adjust seasoning if needed.
8. Serve and enjoy.

NUTRITION: Calories: 227 Fat: 14.8g Carbs: 10g Protein: 18.1g

80. **Bacon Chowder**

Preparation Time: 5 minutes

Cooking Time: 15 minutes

Servings: 6

INGREDIENTS:

- 1-pound bacon strips, chopped
- 1/4 cup chopped onion
- 1 can (12 ounces) evaporated milk
- 1 sprig parsley, chopped

DIRECTIONS:

1. Place the bacon in a skillet then cook over medium heat until it becomes crispy, stirring intermittently.
2. Take out with a slotted spoon; allow to drain on paper towels.
3. Get rid of drippings, reserving 1-1/2 teaspoons in the pan. Put onion to drippings; cook and stir over medium-high heat until tender.
4. Meanwhile, place all ingredients. Boil over high heat.
5. Then reduce heat to medium; cook, uncovered, 10-15 minutes or until tender—Reserve 1 cup potato water.
6. Add milk, salt, and pepper to the saucepan; heat through. Stir in bacon and onion.

NUTRITION Calories: 322 Fat: 31.9g Carbs: 5.4 Protein: 10g

81. **Mexican Soup**

Preparation Time: 5 minutes

Cooking Time: 25 minutes

Servings: 4

INGREDIENTS:

- 1-pound boneless skinless chicken thighs, cut into 3/4-inch pieces
- 1 tablespoon reduced-sodium taco seasoning
- 1 cup salsa
- 1 carton (32 ounces) reduced-sodium chicken broth

DIRECTIONS:

1. Pour oil into a huge saucepan and let it heat over medium-high fire.
2. Add the chicken; cook and stir for 6-8 minutes or until no longer pink. Stir in taco seasoning.
3. Bring the rest of the ingredients to boil. Reduce the heat; simmer, uncover for 5 minutes to allow flavors to blend.
4. Skim fat before serving.

NUTRITION: Calories: 281 Fat: 16.5g Carbs: 5.6g Protein: 25g

82. <u>Mushroom Soup</u>

Preparation time: 10 minutes

Cooking time: 35 minutes

Servings: 8

INGREDIENTS:

- 1-pound baby portobello mushrooms, chopped
- 2 tablespoons olive oil
- 1 carton (32 ounces) reduced-sodium beef broth
- 2 cups heavy whipping cream

DIRECTIONS:

1. In a Dutch oven, sauté mushrooms in oil and butter until tender.
2. Add the contents of seasoning packets, broth, and water. Boil them.
3. Reduce the heat; put a cover and simmer for about 25 minutes.
4. Add cream and heat through.

NUTRITION: Calories: 280 Fat: 26g Carbs: 3.6g Protein: 8g

83. <u>Rustic Beef Soup</u>

Preparation Time: 5 minutes

Cooking Time: 20 minutes

Servings: 4

INGREDIENTS:

- 3 cups beef broth
- 2 cups of frozen mixed vegetables
- 1 teaspoon ground mustard
- Beef roast

DIRECTIONS:

1. In a huge saucepan, combine all the ingredients.
2. Bring to a boil.

3. Reduce heat; simmer, uncovered, for 15-20 minutes or until barley is tender.

NUTRITION: Calories: 450 Fat: 24g Carbs: 8g Protein: 51g

84. <u>Coconut Cauliflower Soup</u>

Preparation Time: 10 minutes

Cooking Time: 26 minutes

Servings: 10

INGREDIENTS:

- 1 medium onion, finely chopped
- 3 tablespoons yellow curry paste
- 2 medium heads cauliflower, broken into florets
- 1 carton (32 ounces) vegetable broth
- 1 cup of coconut milk

DIRECTIONS:

1. In a huge saucepan, heat oil over medium fire. Add onion; cook and stir until softened, 2-3 minutes.
2. Add curry paste; cook until fragrant, 1-2 minutes.
3. Add cauliflower and broth. Increase heat to high; bring to a boil. Reduce heat to medium-low; cook, covered, about 20 minutes.
4. Stir in coconut milk; cook an additional minute.
5. Remove from heat; cool slightly.
6. Pound in batches in a blender or food processor.
7. If desired, top with minced fresh cilantro.

NUTRITION: Facts Calories: 111 Fat: 8g Carbs: 10g Protein: 3g

85. <u>Clam Chowder</u>

Preparation Time: 0 minutes

Cooking Time: 10 minutes

Servings: 5

INGREDIENTS:

- 1 can (10-3/4 ounces) condensed cream of celery soup, undiluted
- 2 cups half-and-half cream
- 2 cans (6-1/2 ounces each) minced/chopped clams, drained
- 1/4 teaspoon ground nutmeg

DIRECTIONS:

1. In a large saucepan, combine all ingredients. Cook and mix over medium heat until heated through.

NUTRITION: Calories: 251 Fat: 14g Carbs: 3.8g Protein: 10g

SNACKS

86. Buttery Slow-Cooker Mushrooms

Preparation Time: 10 minutes

Cooking Time: 4 hours

Servings: 2

INGREDIENTS:

- 6 tablespoons butter
- 1 tablespoon packaged dry ranch dressing mix
- 8 ounces fresh cremini mushrooms
- 2 tablespoons grated Parmesan cheese
- 1 tablespoon chopped fresh flat-leaf Italian parsley

DIRECTIONS:

2. With the crock insert in place, preheat the slow cooker to low.
3. Put the dry ranch dressing and the butter in the bottom of the slow cooker, and allow the butter to melt. Stir to blend the dressing mix and butter.
4. Put the mushrooms into the slow cooker, and stir to coat with the butter-dressing mixture. Sprinkle the top with the Parmesan cheese.
5. Put on the cover of the crockpot and cook on low for 4 hours.
6. Use a slotted spoon to transfer the mushrooms to a serving dish. Top with the chopped parsley and serve.

NUTRITION: Calories: 351 cal Fat: 36g Carbs: 5g Protein: 6g Fiber: 1g

87. Parmesan And Pork Rind Green Beans

Preparation Time: 5 minutes

Cooking Time: 15 minutes

Servings: 2

INGREDIENTS:

- ½ pound fresh green beans
- 2 tablespoons crushed pork rinds
- 2 tablespoons olive oil
- 1 tablespoon grated Parmesan cheese
- Pink Himalayan salt
- Freshly ground black pepper

DIRECTIONS:

1. Preheat the oven to 400°F.
2. In a bowl, mix the green beans, pork rinds, olive oil, and Parmesan cheese. Season with pink Himalayan salt and pepper, and toss until the beans are thoroughly coated.
3. Spread the bean mixture on a baking sheet in a single layer and roast for about 15 minutes. At the halfway point, give the pan a little shake to move the beans around, or just give them a stir.
4. Divide the beans between two plates and serve.

NUTRITION: Calories: 175 cal Fat: 15g Carbs: 8g Protein: 6g Fiber: 3g

88. Crunchy Pork Rind Zucchini Sticks

Preparation Time: 5 minutes

Cooking Time: 25 minutes

Servings: 2

INGREDIENTS:

- 2 medium zucchini, halved lengthwise and seeded
- ¼ cup crushed pork rinds
- ¼ cup grated Parmesan cheese
- 2 garlic cloves, minced
- 2 tablespoons melted butter
- Pink Himalayan salt
- Freshly ground black pepper

- Olive oil, for drizzling

DIRECTIONS:

1. Preheat the oven to 400°F.
2. Line a baking sheet using a silicone baking mat or aluminum foil.
3. Place the zucchini halves cut-side up on the prepared baking sheet.
4. In a bowl, combine the pork rinds, Parmesan cheese, garlic, and melted butter, and season with pink Himalayan salt and pepper. Mix until well combined.
5. Spoon the pork-rind mixture onto each zucchini stick, and drizzle each with a little olive oil.
6. Bake the mixture for about 20 minutes, or until the topping is golden brown.
7. Turn on the broiler to finish browning the zucchini sticks, 3 to 5 minutes, and serve.

NUTRITION: Calories: 231 cal Fat: 20g Carbs: 8g Protein: 9g Fiber: 2g

89. **Keto Bread**

Preparation Time: 5 minutes

Cooking Time: 25 minutes

Servings: 12 slices

INGREDIENTS:

- 5 tablespoons butter, at room temperature, divided
- 6 large eggs, lightly beaten
- 1½ cups almond flour
- 3 teaspoons baking powder
- 1 scoop MCT oil powder (optional, but it is flavorless and adds high-quality fats; I use Perfect Keto's MCT oil powder)
- Pinch pink Himalayan salt

DIRECTIONS:

1. Preheat the oven to 390°F. Coat a 9-by-5-inch of loaf pan with a tablespoon of butter.

2. In a large bowl, utilize a hand mixer to mix the eggs, almond flour, remaining 4 tablespoons of butter, baking powder, MCT oil powder (if using), and pink Himalayan salt until thoroughly blended. Pour into the prepared pan.
3. Bake it for approximately 25 minutes or until a toothpick inserted in the center comes out clean.
4. Slice and serve.

NUTRITION: Calories: 165 cal Fat: 15g Carbs: 4g Protein: 6g Fiber: 2g

90. **Chicken-Pecan Salad Cucumber Bites**

Preparation Time: 15 minutes

Cooking Time: 0 minute

Servings: 2

INGREDIENTS:

- 1 cup diced cooked chicken breast
- 2 tablespoons mayonnaise
- ¼ cup chopped pecans
- ¼ cup diced celery
- Pink Himalayan salt
- Freshly ground black pepper
- 1 cucumber, peeled and cut into ¼-inch slices

DIRECTIONS:

1. In a bowl, mix together the chicken, mayonnaise, pecans, and celery. Season with pink Himalayan salt and pepper.
2. Lay the cucumber slices out on a plate, and add a pinch of pink Himalayan salt to each.
3. Put a spoonful of the chicken-salad mixture on top of each cucumber slice and serve.

NUTRITION: Calories: 323 cal Fat: 24g Carbs: 6g Protein: 23g Fiber: 3g

91. **Buffalo Chicken Dip**

Preparation Time: 10 minutes

Cooking Time: 20 minutes

Servings: 2

INGREDIENTS:

- 1 large cooked boneless chicken breast, shredded
- Butter or olive oil
- 8 ounces cream cheese
- ½ cup shredded Cheddar cheese
- ½ cup chunky blue cheese dressing
- ¼ cup buffalo wing sauce (I use Frank's RedHot Sauce)

DIRECTIONS:

1. Preheat the oven to 375°F. Grease a small baking pan.
2. In a bowl, combine together the chicken, cream cheese, Cheddar cheese, blue cheese dressing, and wing sauce. Move the mixture into the prepared baking pan.
3. Bake for 20 minutes.
4. Pour into a dip dish and serve hot.

NUTRITION: Calories: 859 cal Fat: 73g Carbs: 8g Protein: 41g Fiber: 0g

92. **Roasted Brussels Sprouts With Bacon**

Preparation Time: 5 minutes

Cooking Time: 25 minutes

Servings: 2

INGREDIENTS:

- ½ pound Brussels sprouts, cleaned, trimmed, and halved
- 1 tablespoon olive oil
- Pink Himalayan salt
- Freshly ground black pepper
- 1 teaspoon red pepper flakes
- 6 bacon slices
- 1 tablespoon grated Parmesan cheese

DIRECTIONS:

1. Preheat the oven to 400°F.
2. In a bowl, mix the Brussels sprouts with the olive oil, season with pink Himalayan salt and pepper, then sprinkle the red pepper flakes.
3. Cut the bacon strips into 1-inch pieces. (I use kitchen shears.)
4. Place the Brussels sprouts and bacon on a baking sheet in a single layer. Roast for about 25 minutes. About halfway through the baking time, give the pan a little shake to move the sprouts around, or give them a stir. You want your Brussels sprouts crispy and browned on the outside.
5. Remove the Brussels sprouts from the oven. Divide them between two plates, top each serving with Parmesan cheese, and serve.

NUTRITION: Calories: 248 cal Fat: 18g Carbs: 11g Protein: 14g Fiber: 5g

93. **Salami, Pepperoncini, And Cream Cheese Pinwheels**

Preparation Time: 20 minutes

Cooking Time: 6 hours to chill

Servings: 2

INGREDIENTS:

- 8 ounces cream cheese, at room temperature
- ¼ pound salami, thinly sliced
- 2 tablespoons sliced pepperoncini (I use Mezzetta)

DIRECTIONS:

1. Layout a sheet of plastic wrap on a large cutting board or counter.
2. Place the cream cheese in the center of the plastic wrap, and then add another layer of plastic wrap on top. Using a rolling pin, roll

the cream cheese until it is even and about ¼ inch thick. Try to make the shape somewhat resemble a rectangle.

3. Pull off the top layer of plastic wrap.

4. Place the salami slices so they overlap to cover the cream cheese layer completely.

5. Put a fresh piece of plastic wrap over the salami layer so that you can flip over your cream cheese–salami rectangle. Flip the layer, so the cream cheese side is up.

6. Remove the plastic wrap and add the sliced pepperoncini in a layer on top.

7. Roll the layered ingredients into a tight log, pressing the meat and cream cheese together. (You want it as tight as possible.) Then wrap the roll with plastic wrap and refrigerate for at least 6 hours so it will set.

8. Utilize a very sharp knife to slice the log into slices and serve.

NUTRITION: Calories: 583 cal Fat: 54g Carbs: 7g Protein: 19g Fiber: 0g

94. Bacon-Wrapped Jalapeños

Preparation Time: 10 minutes

Cooking Time: 20 minutes

Servings: 4

INGREDIENTS:

- 10 jalapeños
- 8 ounces cream cheese, at room temperature
- 1 pound bacon (you will use about half a slice per popper)

DIRECTIONS:

1. Preheat the oven to 450°F. Line a baking sheet using aluminum foil or a silicone baking mat.

2. Halve the jalapeños lengthwise, and remove the seeds and membranes (if you like the extra heat, leave them in). Place them on the prepared pan cut-side up.

3. Spread some of the cream cheese inside each jalapeño half.

4. Wrap a jalapeño half with a slice of bacon (depending on the size of the jalapeño, use a whole slice of bacon, or half).

5. Secure the bacon around each jalapeño with 1 to 2 toothpicks, so it stays put while baking.

6. Bake for approximately 20 minutes, or only until the bacon is done and crispy.

7. Serve hot or at room temperature. Either way, they are delicious!

NUTRITION: Calories: 164 cal Fat: 13g Carbs: 1g Protein: 9g Fiber: 0g

95. Creamy Broccoli-Bacon Salad

Preparation Time: 10 minutes

Cooking Time: 10 minutes

Servings: 2

INGREDIENTS:

- 6 bacon slices
- ½ pound fresh broccoli, cut into small florets
- ¼ cup sliced almonds
- ⅓ cup mayonnaise
- 1 tablespoon honey mustard dressing

DIRECTIONS:

1. Place the bacon in a huge skillet over medium-high heat, cook on both sides until crispy, about 8 minutes.

2. Move the bacon to a towel-lined plate to drain and cool for 5 minutes. When cool, break the bacon into crumbles.

3. In a huge bowl, mix the broccoli with the almonds and bacon.

4. In a bowl, stir the mayonnaise and honey mustard together.

5. Put the dressing unto the broccoli salad, and toss to combine thoroughly.

6. Let the salad chill for an hour or more before serving.

NUTRITION: Calories: 549 cal Fat: 49g Carbs: 16g Protein: 16g Fiber: 5g

96. Cauliflower Steaks With Bacon And Blue Cheese

Preparation Time: 5 minutes

Cooking Time: 20 minutes

Servings: 2

INGREDIENTS:

- ½ head cauliflower
- 1 tablespoon olive oil
- Pink Himalayan salt
- Freshly ground black pepper
- 4 bacon slices
- 2 tablespoons blue cheese salad dressing (I use Trader Joe's Chunky Blue Cheese Dressing)

DIRECTIONS:

1. Preheat the oven to 425°F.
2. Get a baking sheet lined with aluminum foil or a silicone baking mat.
3. To prepare the cauliflower steaks, remove and discard the leaves and cut the cauliflower into 1-inch-thick slices. You can also roast the extra floret crumbles that fall off with the steaks.
4. Place the cauliflower steaks on the prepared baking sheet, and brush with the olive oil. You want the surface just lightly coated with the oil, so it gets caramelized—season with pink Himalayan pepper and salt. Put the bacon slices on the pan, together with the cauliflower floret crumbles.
5. Roast the cauliflower steaks for 20 minutes.
6. Place the cauliflower steaks on two plates. Sprinkle with blue cheese dressing, top with crumbled bacon, and serve.

NUTRITION: Calories: 254 cal Fat: 19g Carbs: 11g Protein: 11g Fiber: 4g

97. Cauliflower "Potato" Salad

Preparation Time: 10 minutes and 3 hours to chill

Cooking Time: 25 minutes

Servings: 2

INGREDIENTS:

- ½ head cauliflower
- 1 tablespoon olive oil
- Pink Himalayan salt
- Freshly ground black pepper
- ⅓ cup mayonnaise
- 1 tablespoon mustard
- ¼ cup diced dill pickles
- 1 teaspoon paprika

DIRECTIONS:

1. Preheat the oven to 400°F. Line a baking sheet using aluminum foil or a silicone baking mat.
2. Cut the cauliflower into 1-inch pieces.
3. Place the cauliflower inside a large bowl, add the olive oil, season with the pink Himalayan salt and pepper, and toss to combine.
4. Spread out the cauliflower on the baking sheet you prepared and bake for 25 minutes, or just until the cauliflower begins to brown. In the middle the cooking time, give the pan a couple of shakes or stir so all sides of the cauliflower cook.
5. In a huge bowl, mix the cauliflower together with the mayonnaise, mustard, and pickles. Sprinkle the paprika on top, and chill in the refrigerator for 3 hours before serving.

NUTRITION: Calories: 386 cal Fat: 37g Carbs: 13g Protein: 5g Fiber: 5g

DESSERTS

98. Coconut Bombs

Preparation Time: 30 minutes

Cooking Time: 15 minutes

Servings: 6

INGREDIENTS:

- 4 oz. flaked coconut
- ¼ cup coconut oil, melted
- ¼ tsp. vanilla paste
- 20 drops stevia

DIRECTIONS:

1. Preheat oven to 350°F. And line baking sheet with parchment paper. Spread over coconut flakes and put them in the oven.
2. Toast the flakes for 5-8 minutes until golden. Stir once to prevent burning.
3. Move them to a blender and pulse until smooth.
4. Add the coconut oil, vanilla paste, and stevia. Stir to combine.
5. Divide among 12 mini paper cases and put them in the freezer for 30 minutes.

NUTRITION: Calories:145 Fat: 15.4 Carbohydrates: 2.9 Protein:1

99. Raspberry Cheesecake

Preparation Time: 10 minutes

Cooking Time: 25 minutes

Servings: 6

INGREDIENTS:

- 2/3 cup coconut oil, melted
- ½ cup cream cheese
- 6 eggs
- 3 tbsp. granulated sweetener
- 1 tsp. vanilla extract
- ½ tsp. baking powder
- ¾ cup raspberries

DIRECTIONS:

1. Preheat the oven to 350° F. Get a baking dish that's lined with parchment paper and set aside.
2. In a bowl, mix the coconut oil and cream cheese together until smooth.
3. Beat in eggs, then beat in the sweetener, vanilla, and baking powder until smooth.
4. Transfer the batter, using spoon, into the baking dish and smooth out the top. Scatter the raspberries on top.
5. Bake for about 25 to 30 minutes or up until the center is firm.

NUTRITION: Calories:176 Fat: 18 Carbohydrates: 3 Protein:6

100. Keto Chocolate Nut Clusters

Preparation Time: 5 minutes

Cooking Time: 10 minutes

Servings: 25

INGREDIENTS:

- 9 oz. sugar-free dark chocolate chips
- ¼ cup unrefined coconut oil
- 2 cups salted mixed nuts

DIRECTIONS:

1. Line a rimmed baking sheet using a parchment paper or a silicone baking mat.
2. In a microwave-safe bowl, put a piece of the chocolate chips and coconut oil and microwave till the chocolate is melted.
3. Use a spatula to mix. Let it cool handiest to some degree before using it.
4. Mix till everything of the nuts is overlaying inside the chocolate.
5. Drop a huge spoonful of the combo onto the prepared preparing sheet.

6. Store scraps in the refrigerator for up to three weeks.

NUTRITION: Calories:170 Fat: 15 Carbohydrates: 3 Protein:3

101. Cocoa Coconut Butter Fat Bombs

Preparation Time: 5 minutes

Cooking Time: 10 minutes

Servings: 12

INGREDIENTS:

- 1 cup of coconut oil
- ½ cup unsalted butter
- 6 tbsp. unsweetened cocoa powder
- 15 drops liquid stevia
- ½ cup coconut butter

DIRECTIONS:

1. In a saucepan, put butter, coconut oil, cocoa powder, and stevia and cook over low heat, frequently stirring until melted.
2. Melt coconut butter in another saucepan over low heat.
3. Pour 2 tbsp. of the cocoa mixture into each well of a 12-cup silicone mold.
4. Add 1 tbsp. of melted coconut butter to each well.
5. Put in the freezer until hardened, about 30 minutes.

NUTRITION: Calories: 297 Fat: 30 Carbohydrates: 4 Protein:3

102. Blueberry Lemon Cake

Preparation Time: 10 minutes

Cooking Time: 40 minutes

Servings: 4

INGREDIENTS:

- For the Cake:
- 2/3 cup almond flour
- 5 eggs

- ⅓ cup almond milk, unsweetened
- ¼ cup erythritol
- 2 tsp. vanilla extract
- Juice of 2 lemons
- 1 tsp. lemon zest
- ½ tsp. baking soda
- Pinch of salt
- ½ cup fresh blueberries
- 2 tbsp. butter, Melted
- For the Frosting:
- ½ cup heavy cream
- Juice of 1 lemon
- 1/8 cup erythritol

DIRECTIONS:

1. Preheat the oven to 35° F.
2. In a bowl, add the almond flour, eggs, and almond milk and mix well until smooth.
3. Add the erythritol, a pinch of salt, baking soda, lemon zest, lemon juice, and vanilla extract. Mix and combine well.
4. Fold in the blueberries.
5. Use the butter to grease the springform pans.
6. Pour the batter into the greased pans.
7. Put on a baking sheet for even baking.
8. Put in the oven to bake until cooked through in the middle and slightly brown on the top, about 35 to 40 minutes.
9. Let cool before removing from the pan.
10. Mix the erythritol, lemon juice, and heavy cream. Mix well.
11. Pour frosting on top.

NUTRITION: Calories: 274 Fat: 23 Carbohydrates: 8 Protein: 9

103. Rich Chocolate Mousse

Preparation Time: 10 minutes

Cooking Time: 15 minutes

Servings: 3

Ingredients:

- ¼ cup low-fat coconut cream
- 2 cups fat-free Greek-style yogurt, strained
- 4 tsp. powered cocoa, no added sugar
- 2 tbsp. stevia/xylitol/bacon syrup
- 1 tsp. natural vanilla extract

DIRECTIONS:

1. In a medium mixing bowl, place all of the ingredients and mix well.
2. Put individual serving bowls or glasses and refrigerate them. Serve cold

NUTRITION: Calories: 269 Fat: 3 Carbohydrates: 20 Protein: 43

104. Home Made Coconut Ice Cream

Preparation Time: 10 minutes

Cooking Time: 95 minutes

Servings: 4

INGREDIENTS:

- 2 cups evaporated low-fat milk
- ⅓ cup low-fat condensed milk
- 1 cup low-fat coconut milk
- ½ cup stevia/xylitol/bacon syrup
- 2 scoops whey protein concentrate
- 2 tsp. sugar-free coconut extract
- 1 Tsp. Dried Coconut

DIRECTIONS:

1. Place all of the ingredients in a medium-sized mixing bowl and combine well.
2. Heat the mixture over medium heat until it starts to bubble.
3. Take it away from heat and let the mixture cool down.
4. Chill mixture for about an hour, then freeze in ice cream maker as outlined by the manufacturer's directions.

NUTRITION: Calories: 182 Fat: 2 Carbohydrates: 20 Protein: 22

105. Berries with Coconut Cream

Preparation Time: 5 minutes

Cooking Time: 15 minutes

Servings: 2

INGREDIENTS:

- 1 cup fat-free cream cheese
- ¼ cup coconut chunks
- ½ tsp. sugar-free coconut extract
- ½ cup mixed berries
- 3 tsp. stevia/xylitol/yacon syrup

DIRECTIONS:

1. Beat cream cheese until fluffy.
2. Put the coconut chunks and stevia inside a blender and puree.
3. Combine using the Cream cheese and set in serving plates. Top with berries.

NUTRITION: Calories :200 Fat: 4 Carbohydrates:17 Protein: 22

106. Coconut Panna Cotta

Preparation Time: 5 minutes

Cooking Time: 20 minutes

Servings: 2

INGREDIENTS:

- 2 cups skimmed milk
- 1/2 cup water
- 1 tsp. sugar-free coconut extract
- 1 envelope powdered grass-fed – organic gelatin – sugar-free
- 2 scoops whey protein isolate
- 4 tbsp. stevia/xylitol/yacon syrup
- ⅓ cup fresh raspberries
- 2 tbsp. fresh mint

DIRECTIONS:

1. In a non-stick pan, pour the milk, stevia, water, and coconut extract.

2. Bring to a boil.
3. Slowly add the gelatin and stir well until the mixtures start to thicken.
4. When ready, divide the mix among the small silicon cups.
5. Refrigerate overnight to relax and hang up.
6. Remove through the fridge and thoroughly turn each cup over ahead of a serving plate.
7. Garnish with raspberries and fresh Mint, serve and revel in.

NUTRITION: Calories:130 Fat: 3 Carbohydrates: 14 Protein: 29

107. Lemon & Lime Sorbet

Preparation Time: 5 minutes

Cooking Time: 120 minutes

Servings: 2

INGREDIENTS:

- 1 cup of water
- ¾ cup stevia/xylitol/yacon syrup
- 1 cup fresh lemon juice
- 2 scoops whey protein concentrate 1/2 cup lime juice
- 4 whole lemons or oranges cut in half; flesh removed

DIRECTIONS:

1. Put the lake, stevia, lemon, and lime juice into a blender and puree.
2. Move the mixture into a container and freeze for about a couple of hours.
3. Remove from the freezer and puree once more using a blender.
4. Put inside an airtight container and return to freezer.
5. Serve in lemon/orange cups and garnish with fresh mint.

NUTRITION: Calories:150 Fat: 1 Carbohydrates: 9 Protein: 25

108. Avocado Kale Keto Bowl

Preparation Time: 10 minutes

Cooking Time: 0 minutes

Servings: 2

INGREDIENTS:

- ½ avocado, sliced
- 1 cup kale leaves
- 1 banana, sliced
- ½ cup raspberries
- 1 cup almond milk
- 1 kiwi, sliced
- 2 drops stevia
- ½ cup ice
- 1 tsp chia seeds

DIRECTION:

1. Place avocado, kale, stevia, banana, almond milk, and ice in a blender. Process until smooth and creamy.
2. Transfer to a bowl.
3. Serve and decorate the bowl by placing chia seeds, kiwi, and raspberries.

NUTRITION: Calories: 230 Fat: 1 Carbohydrates: 12 Protein: 15

109. Mozzarella Sticks

Preparation Time: 8 minutes

Cooking Time: 2 minutes

Servings: 2

INGREDIENTS:

- 1 large whole egg
- 3 sticks mozzarella cheese in half (Overnight frozen)
- 2 tablespoon grated parmesan cheese
- 1/2 cup almond flour
- 1/4 cup coconut oil
- 2 1/2 teaspoons Italian seasoning blend
- 1 tablespoon chopped parsley
- 1/2 teaspoon salt

DIRECTIONS:

1. Get a cast-iron skillet and put the coconut oil. Heat it over low to medium heat.
2. Crack the egg in a small bowl in the meantime and beat it well.
3. Take another bowl of medium size and add parmesan cheese, almond flour, and seasonings to it. Whisk together the ingredients until a smooth mixture is prepared.
4. Take the overnight frozen mozzarella stick and dip in the beaten egg, then coat it well with the dry mixture. Do the same with all the remaining cheese sticks.
5. Place all the coated sticks in the preheated skillet and cook them for 2 minutes or until they start giving a golden-brown look from all sides.
6. Remove from the skillet once cooked properly and place over paper towel so that any extra oil gets absorbed.
7. Sprinkle parsley over the sticks if you desire and serve with keto marinara sauce.

NUTRITION: Calories: 430 Fat: 39 Carbohydrates: 10 Protein: 20

110. Avocado Taco Boats

Preparation Time: 5 minutes

Cooking Time: 20 minutes

Servings: 4

INGREDIENTS:

- 4 grape tomatoes
- 2 large avocados
- 1 lbs. ground beef
- 4 tablespoon taco seasoning
- 3/4 cup shredded sharp cheddar cheese
- 4 slices pickled jalapeño
- 1/4 cup salsa
- 3 shredded romaine leaves
- 1/4 cup sour cream
- 2/3 cup water

DIRECTIONS:

1. Take a skillet of considerable size, grease it with oil, and heat it over medium-high heat. Cook the ground beef in it for 10-15 minutes or until it gives a brownish look.
2. Once the beef gets brown, drain the grease from the skillet and add the water and the taco seasoning.
3. Reduce the heat once the taco seasoning gets mixed well and simmer for 8-10 minutes.
4. Take both avocados and prepare their halves using a sharp knife.
5. Take each avocado shell and fill it with ¼ of the shredded romaine leaves.
6. Fill each shell with ¼ of the cooked ground beef.
7. Do the topping with sour cream, cheese, jalapeno, salsa, and tomato before you serve the delicious avocado taco boats.

NUTRITION: Calories: 430 Fat: 35 Carbohydrates: 5 Protein: 32

111. Cheesy Biscuits

Preparation Time: 20 minutes

Cooking Time: 20 minutes

Servings: 9

INGREDIENTS:

- 4 eggs
- 2 cups almond flour
- 2 ½ cups shredded cheddar cheese
- 1/4 cup half-and-half
- 1 tablespoon baking powder

DIRECTIONS:

1. Preheat oven to 350°F and get the baking sheet ready by lining it with parchment paper.
2. Take a large bowl and mix the baking powder and almond flour in that.
3. Add cheddar cheese to the mixture and mix until well combined.

4. Take a small bowl, add half and half, and also crack the eggs into it. Mix well until thoroughly blended.

5. Put the egg mixture into the flour mixture and keep whisking with the help of a spatula to prepare a smooth batter.

6. Take portions of the batter using a scoop and put them on the baking sheet. Make sure that you take the portions in exact sizes and flatten them a bit from the top.

7. Place the baking sheet in the preheated oven and bake for 20 minutes or until the time you get a golden-brown look.

8. Take away from the oven once done baking and transfer to the wire rack to cool before serving.

NUTRITION: Calories: 320   Fat: 27
Carbohydrates: 8 Protein: 15

30-DAY MEAL PLAN

	BREAKFAST	LUNCH	DINNER	DESSERT/ SNACK
DAY 1	PEANUT BUTTER CUP SMOOTHIE	VERDE CHICKEN ENCHILADAS	LEMON BUTTER PORK CHOPS	COCONUT BOMBS
DAY 2	BERRY GREEN SMOOTHIE	KETO FRIED CHICKEN	BACON WRAPPED CHICKEN WITH GRILLED ASPARAGUS	BUTTERY SLOW-COOKER MUSHROOMS
DAY 3	LEMON-CASHEW SMOOTHIE	TURKEY TACO BOATS	GRILLED SANDWICH CHEESE	PARMESAN AND PORK RIND GREEN BEANS
DAY 4	SPINACH-BLUEBERRY SMOOTHIE	ALEX'S "CHICK AND BROCK" CASSEROLE	SPINACH CHICKEN CHEESY BAKE	CRUNCHY PORK RIND ZUCCHINI STICKS
DAY 5	CREAMY CINNAMON SMOOTHIE	STUFFED CHICKEN FOR SUPPAH	FULLY LOADED BURGER BOWLS	KETO BREAD
DAY 6	NUT MEDLEY GRANOLA	SILKY CHICKEN WITH MUSHROOM SAUCE	ROASTED LAMB RACK	KETO CHOCOLATE NUT CLUSTERS
DAY 7	BACON-ARTICHOKE OMELET	INDOOR BBQ CHICKEN	PARMESAN WINGS WITH YOGURT SAUCE	COCOA COCONUT BUTTER FAT BOMBS
DAY 8	MUSHROOM FRITTATA	CHIPOTLE CHICKEN FAJITA BOWL	ZINGY TUNA STEAKS WITH SPINACH	BLUEBERRY LEMON CAKE
DAY 9	BREAKFAST	FLUFFY	BRAISED BEEF	CHICKEN-PECAN

	BAKE	CHICKEN	BRISKET	SALAD CUCUMBER BITES
DAY 10	AVOCADO AND EGGS	STUFFED CHICKEN FOR SUPPAH	BEEF CHUCK ROAST	RICH CHOCOLATE MOUSSE
DAY 11	PEANUT BUTTER CUP SMOOTHIE	N'AWLINS CHICKEN	CORN AND BACON CHOWDER	ROASTED BRUSSELS SPROUTS WITH BACON
DAY 12	NUT MEDLEY GRANOLA	FOUR HORSEMEN BUTTER CHICKEN	PORK SHIITAKE WITH "FAST KIMCHI" STIR FRY	HOMEMADE COCONUT ICE CREAM
DAY 13	BERRY GREEN SMOOTHIE	TURKEY TACO BOATS	CREAMY PORK TENDERLOIN	BERRIES WITH COCONUT CREAM
DAY 14	BACON-ARTICHOKE OMELET	ALEX'S "CHICK AND BROCK" CASSEROLE	CHICKEN, BROCCOLI & CASHEW STIR-FRY	SALAMI, PEPPERONCINI, AND CREAM CHEESE PINWHEELS
DAY 15	LEMON-CASHEW SMOOTHIE	STUFFED CHICKEN FOR SUPPAH	CHICKEN DRUMSTICKS IN TOMATO SAUCE	BACON-WRAPPED JALAPEÑOS
DAY 16	CREAMY CINNAMON SMOOTHIE	SILKY CHICKEN WITH MUSHROOM SAUCE	ITALIAN SAUSAGE SATAY	AVOCADO KALE KETO BOWL
DAY 17	NUT MEDLEY GRANOLA	INDOOR BBQ CHICKEN	SEASONED PORK CHOPS	LEMON & LIME SORBET
DAY 18	BACON-ARTICHOKE OMELET	VERDE CHICKEN ENCHILADAS	SPICED PORK TENDERLOIN	CAULIFLOWER "POTATO" SALAD
DAY 19	MUSHROOM FRITTATA	KETO FRIED CHICKEN	CREAMY STUFFED CHICKEN	CREAMY BROCCOLI-BACON SALAD

			WITH PARMA HAM	
DAY 20	BREAKFAST BAKE	TURKEY TACO BOATS	SHERRY AND BUTTER PRAWNS	AVOCADO TACO BOATS
DAY 21	PEANUT BUTTER CUP SMOOTHIE	RICH AND SPICY SEAFOOD STEW	BACON CHOWDER	MOZZARELLA STICKS
DAY 22	NUT MEDLEY GRANOLA	TILAPIA WITH SPICY DIJON SAUCE	GARLICKY PORK ROAST	CHEESY BISCUITS
DAY 23	BERRY GREEN SMOOTHIE	FAMILY SEAFOOD BOWL	FULLY LOADED BURGER BOWLS	COCOA COCONUT BUTTER FAT BOMBS
DAY 24	BACON-ARTICHOKE OMELET	RED SNAPPER SOUP	LEMON THREADED CHICKEN SKEWERS	RASPBERRY CHEESECAKE
DAY 25	LEMON-CASHEW SMOOTHIE	MIDDLE-EASTERN SALMON WITH NABULSI	TILAPIA WITH SPICY DIJON SAUCE	COCONUT PANNA COTTA
DAY 26	NUT MEDLEY GRANOLA	AMBERJACK FILLETS WITH CHEESE SAUCE	BASIL-RUBBED PORK CHOPS	SALAMI, PEPPERONCINI, AND CREAM CHEESE PINWHEELS
DAY 27	BACON-ARTICHOKE OMELET	CLAMS WITH GARLIC-TOMATO SAUCE	SPLENDID JALAPENO POPPERS	BACON-WRAPPED JALAPEÑOS
DAY 28	MUSHROOM FRITTATA	SHERRY AND BUTTER PRAWNS	EGGPLANT & TOMATO BRAISED CHICKEN	AVOCADO KALE KETO BOWL
DAY 29	BREAKFAST	EASY	BEEF CHUCK	LEMON & LIME

	BAKE	HALIBUT STEAKS	ROAST	SORBET
DAY 30	AVOCADO AND EGGS	CHEESY TUNA PÂTÉ	SPINACH CHICKEN CHEESY BAKE	BERRIES WITH COCONUT CREAM
	BREAKFAST	LUNCH	DINNER	DESSERT/ SNACK
DAY 1	PEANUT BUTTER CUP SMOOTHIE	VERDE CHICKEN ENCHILADAS	EASY HALIBUT STEAKS	COCONUT BOMBS
DAY 2	BERRY GREEN SMOOTHIE	KETO FRIED CHICKEN	BACON WRAPPED CHICKEN WITH GRILLED ASPARAGUS	BUTTERY SLOW-COOKER MUSHROOMS
DAY 3	ALMOND BUTTER MUFFINS	KETO BROCCOLI SALAD	LEMON GARLIC SHRIMP PASTA	GRAIN-FREE TORTILLA CHIPS
DAY 4	CLASSIC WESTERN OMELET	KETO SHEET PAN CHICKEN AND RAINBOW VEGGIES	ONE-PAN TEX MEX	CHEESES CHIPS
DAY 5	SHEET PAN EGGS WITH PEPPER JACK AND HAM	SKINNY BANG BANG ZUCCHINI NOODLES	SPINACH ARTICHOKE-STUFFED CHICKEN BREASTS	SNACK PARTIES TREAT
DAY 6	DETOXIFYING GREEN SMOOTHIE	KETO CAESAR SALAD	CHICKEN PARMESAN	SWEET TOOTH CARVING PANA COTTA
DAY 7	NUTTY PUMPKIN SMOOTHIE	KETO BUFFALO CHICKEN EMPANADAS	BLACKENED SALMON WITH AVOCADO SALSA	HALLOWEEN SPECIAL FAT BOMBS

DAY 8	TOMATO MOZZARELLA EGG MUFFINS	PEPPERONI AND CHEDDAR STROMBOLI	BOLOGNESE SAUCE	PRETTY BLUEBERRY BITES
DAY 9	CRISPY CHAI WAFFLES	TUNA CASSEROLE	SHEET PAN JALAPEÑO BURGERS	COLD MINI MUFFINS
DAY 10	CREAMY CHOCOLATE PROTEIN SMOOTHIE	BRUSSELS SPROUT AND HAMBURGER GRATIN	GRILLED HERB GARLIC CHICKEN	CHOCOLATE LOVER'S MUFFINS
DAY 11	KALE AVOCADO SMOOTHIE	COLE SLAW KETO WRAP	LEMON BUTTER FISH	DELIGHTFUL CAULIFLOWER POPPERS
DAY 12	ALMOND BUTTER PROTEIN SMOOTHIE	KETO CHICKEN CLUB LETTUCE WRAP	CHILI LIME COD	DELECTABLE TOMATO SLICES
DAY 13	ALMOND BUTTER MUFFINS	KETO BROCCOLI SALAD	LEMON GARLIC SHRIMP PASTA	GRAIN-FREE TORTILLA CHIPS
DAY 14	CLASSIC WESTERN OMELET	KETO SHEET PAN CHICKEN AND RAINBOW VEGGIES	ONE-PAN TEX MEX	CHEESES CHIPS
DAY 15	SHEET PAN EGGS WITH PEPPER JACK AND HAM	SKINNY BANG BANG ZUCCHINI NOODLES	SPINACH ARTICHOKE-STUFFED CHICKEN BREASTS	SNACK PARTIES TREAT
DAY 16	DETOXIFYING GREEN SMOOTHIE	KETO CAESAR SALAD	CHICKEN PARMESAN	SWEET TOOTH CARVING PANA COTTA
DAY 17	NUTTY PUMPKIN	KETO BUFFALO	BLACKENED SALMON WITH	HALLOWEEN SPECIAL FAT BOMBS

	SMOOTHIE	CHICKEN EMPANADAS	AVOCADO SALSA	
DAY 18	TOMATO MOZZARELLA EGG MUFFINS	PEPPERONI AND CHEDDAR STROMBOLI	BOLOGNESE SAUCE	PRETTY BLUEBERRY BITES
DAY 19	CRISPY CHAI WAFFLES	TUNA CASSEROLE	SHEET PAN JALAPEÑO BURGERS	COLD MINI MUFFINS
DAY 20	CREAMY CHOCOLATE PROTEIN SMOOTHIE	BRUSSELS SPROUT AND HAMBURGER GRATIN	GRILLED HERB GARLIC CHICKEN	CHOCOLATE LOVER'S MUFFINS
DAY 21	KALE AVOCADO SMOOTHIE	COLE SLAW KETO WRAP	LEMON BUTTER FISH	DELIGHTFUL CAULIFLOWER POPPERS
DAY 22	ALMOND BUTTER PROTEIN SMOOTHIE	KETO CHICKEN CLUB LETTUCE WRAP	CHILI LIME COD	DELECTABLE TOMATO SLICES
DAY 23	ALMOND BUTTER MUFFINS	KETO BROCCOLI SALAD	LEMON GARLIC SHRIMP PASTA	GRAIN-FREE TORTILLA CHIPS
DAY 24	CLASSIC WESTERN OMELET	KETO SHEET PAN CHICKEN AND RAINBOW VEGGIES	ONE-PAN TEX MEX	CHEESES CHIPS
DAY 25	SHEET PAN EGGS WITH PEPPER JACK AND HAM	SKINNY BANG BANG ZUCCHINI NOODLES	SPINACH ARTICHOKE-STUFFED CHICKEN BREASTS	SNACK PARTIES TREAT
DAY 26	DETOXIFYING GREEN SMOOTHIE	KETO CAESAR SALAD	CHICKEN PARMESAN	SWEET TOOTH CARVING PANA COTTA

DAY 27	NUTTY PUMPKIN SMOOTHIE	KETO BUFFALO CHICKEN EMPANADAS	BLACKENED SALMON WITH AVOCADO SALSA	HALLOWEEN SPECIAL FAT BOMBS
DAY 28	TOMATO MOZZARELLA EGG MUFFINS	PEPPERONI AND CHEDDAR STROMBOLI	BOLOGNESE SAUCE	PRETTY BLUEBERRY BITES
DAY 29	CRISPY CHAI WAFFLES	TUNA CASSEROLE	SHEET PAN JALAPEÑO BURGERS	COLD MINI MUFFINS
DAY 30	CREAMY CHOCOLATE PROTEIN SMOOTHIE	BRUSSELS SPROUT AND HAMBURGER GRATIN	GRILLED HERB GARLIC CHICKEN	CHOCOLATE LOVER'S MUFFINS

CONCLUSION

Thanks for downloading this book. It's my firm belief that it will provide you with all the answers to your questions.

When a person finds a keto calculator they like, they will enter their information into the calculator to get their results. These typically ask for gender, height, weight, age, and body mass index to begin the process. Next, they might ask someone to enter their activity level and the end goals of being on a diet, such as losing weight, improving a health condition, or building muscle mass. Once all of these factors have been entered, the calculator determines the macronutrients a person should consume daily. With these numbers, a person can keep a notebook to track their progress throughout the day to meet their goals.

Printed in the USA
CPSIA information can be obtained
at www.ICGtesting.com
LVHW070847100124
768548LV00012B/587